What People Are Saying about Threshold Bible Study

"Stephen Binz's Threshold Bible Study is a marvelous project. With lucidity and creativity, Binz offers today's believing communities a rich and accessible treasury of biblical scholarship. The series' brilliance lies in its simplicity of presentation complemented by critical depth of thought and reflective insight. This is a wonderful gift for personal and communal study, especially for those wishing to make a home for the Word in their hearts."

■ **CAROL J. DEMPSEY**, OP, *Professor of Theology,*
University of Portland, OR

"God's Holy Word addresses the deepest levels of our lives with the assurance of divine grace and wisdom for our individual and communal faith. I am grateful for this new series introducing our Catholic people to the riches of Sacred Scripture. May these guides to understanding the great truths of our Redemption bring us all closer to the Lord of our salvation."

■ *Timothy Cardinal Dolan, Archbishop of New York*

"Threshold Bible Study offers solid scholarship and spiritual depth. Drawing on the Church's living Tradition and the Jewish roots of the New Testament, Threshold Bible Study can be counted on for lively individual study and prayer, even while it offers spiritual riches to deepen communal conversation and reflection among the people of God."

■ **SCOTT HAHN**, *founder of the St. Paul Center*
for Biblical Theology

"Threshold Bible Study is a refreshing approach to enable participants to ponder the Scriptures more deeply. The thematic material is clearly presented with a mix of information and spiritual nourishment. The questions are thoughtful and the principles for group discussion are quite helpful. This series provides a practical way for faithful people to get to know the Bible better and to enjoy the fruits of biblical prayer."

■ **IRENE NOWELL**, OSB, *Mount St. Scholastica,*
Atchison, Kansas

"The distance many feel between the Word of God and their everyday lives can be overwhelming. It need not be so. Threshold Bible Study is a fine blend of the best of biblical scholarship and a realistic sensitivity to the spiritual journey of the believing Christian. I recommend it highly."

■ **FRANCIS J. MOLONEY**, SDB, *Senior Professorial Fellow*
at Australian Catholic University, Melbourne

"Stephen Binz offers an invaluable guide that can make reading the Bible enjoyable (again) and truly nourishing. A real education on how to read the Bible, this series prepares people to discuss Scripture and to share it in community."

■ JACQUES NIEUVIARTS, *Professor of Scripture,*
Institut Catholique de Toulouse, France

"Threshold Bible Study is appropriately named, for its commentary and study questions bring people to the threshold of the text and invite them in. The questions guide but do not dominate. They lead readers to ponder and wrestle with the biblical passages and take them across the threshold toward life with God. Stephen Binz's work stands in the tradition of the biblical renewal movement and brings it back to life. We need more of this in the Church."

■ KATHLEEN M. O'CONNOR, *Professor of Old Testament,*
Columbia Theological Seminary

"I most strongly recommend Stephen Binz's Threshold Bible Study for adult Bible classes, religious education, and personal spiritual enrichment. The series is exceptional for its scholarly solidity, pastoral practicality, and clarity of presentation. The church owes Binz a great debt of gratitude for his generous and competent labor in the service of the Word of God."

■ PETER C. PHAN, *The Ignacio Ellacuria Professor*
of Catholic Social Thought, Georgetown University

"Threshold Bible Study is the perfect series of Bible study books for serious students with limited time. Each lesson is brief, illuminating, challenging, wittily written, and a pleasure to study. The reader will reap a rich harvest of wisdom from the efforts expended."

■ JOHN J. PILCH, *Adjunct Professor of Biblical Studies,*
Georgetown University, Washington, D.C.

"Threshold Bible Study helpfully introduces the lay reader into the life-enhancing process of *Lectio Divina* or prayerful reading of Scripture, individually or in a group. This series, prepared by a reputable biblical scholar and teacher, responds creatively to the exhortation of the Council to provide God's people abundant nourishment from the table of God's word. The process proposed leads the reader from Bible study to personal prayer, community involvement, and active Christian commitment in the world."

■ SANDRA M. SCHNEIDERS, *Professor of New Testament*
and Spirituality, Jesuit School of Theology, Berkeley

THRESHOLD
BIBLE STUDY

JESUS,
the COMPASSIONATE
SAVIOR

PART ONE

Luke
[1–11]

STEPHEN J. BINZ

TWENTY
THIRD 23rd
PUBLICATIONS
NEW LONDON, CT 06320

THIRD PRINTING 2015

TWENTY-THIRD PUBLICATIONS
A Division of Bayard
One Montauk Avenue, Suite 200
New London, CT 06320
(860) 437-3012 or (800) 321-0411
www.23rdpublications.com

ISBN: 978-1-58595-872-6
Library of Congress Control Number: 2012918684
Printed in the U.S.A.

Contents

LESSONS 13–18

LESSONS 19–24

LESSONS 25–30

How to Use
Threshold Bible Study

T hreshold Bible Study is a dynamic, informative, inspiring, and life-changing series that helps you learn about Scripture in a whole new way. Each book will help you explore new dimensions of faith and discover deeper insights for your life as a disciple of Jesus.

The threshold is a place of transition. The threshold of God's word invites you to enter that place where God's truth, goodness, and beauty can shine into your life and fill your mind and heart. Through the Holy Spirit, the threshold becomes holy ground, sacred space, and graced time. God can teach you best at the threshold, because God opens your life to his word and fills you with the Spirit of truth.

With Threshold Bible Study each topic or book of the Bible is approached in a thematic way. You will understand and reflect on the biblical texts through overarching themes derived from biblical theology. Through this method, the study of Scripture will impact your life in a unique way and transform you from within.

These books are designed for maximum flexibility. Each study is presented in a workbook format, with sections for reading, reflecting, writing, discussing, and praying. Each Threshold book contains thirty lessons, which you can use for your daily study over the course of a month or which can be divided into six lessons per week, providing a group study of six weekly sessions (the first session deals with the Introduction). These studies are ideal for Bible study groups, small Christian communities, adult faith formation, student groups, Sunday school, neighborhood groups, and family reading, as well as for individual learning.

The commentary that follows each biblical passage launches your reflection on that passage and helps you begin to see its significance within the context of your contemporary experience. The questions following the commentary challenge you to understand the passage more fully and apply it to your own life. Space for writing after each question is ideal for personal study and also allows group participants to prepare for the weekly discussion. The prayer helps conclude your study each day by integrating your learning into your relationship with God.

The method of Threshold Bible Study is rooted in the ancient tradition of *lectio divina,* whereby studying the Bible becomes a means of deeper intimacy with God and a transformed life. Reading and interpreting the text (*lectio*) is followed by reflective meditation on its message (*meditatio*). This reading and reflecting flows into prayer from the heart (*oratio* and *contemplatio*). In this way, one listens to God through the Scripture and then responds to God in prayer.

This ancient method assures you that Bible study is a matter of both the mind and the heart. It is not just an intellectual exercise to learn more and be able to discuss the Bible with others. It is, more importantly, a transforming experience. Reflecting on God's word, guided by the Holy Spirit, illumines the mind with wisdom and stirs the heart with zeal.

Following the personal Bible study, Threshold Bible Study offers ways to extend personal *lectio divina* into a weekly conversation with others. This communal experience will allow participants to enhance their appreciation of the message and build up a spiritual community (*collatio*). The end result will be to increase not only individual faith but also faithful witness in the context of daily life (*operatio*).

When bringing Threshold Bible Study to a church community, try to make every effort to include as many people as possible. Many will want to study on their own; others will want to study with family, a group of friends, or a few work associates; some may want to commit themselves to share insights through a weekly conference call, daily text messaging, or an online social network; and others will want to gather weekly in established small groups.

By encouraging Threshold Bible Study and respecting the many ways people desire to make Bible study a regular part of their lives, you will widen the number of people in your church community who study the Bible regularly in whatever way they are able in their busy lives. Simply sign up people at the Sunday services and order bulk quantities for your church. Encourage people to follow the daily study as faithfully as they can. This encouragement can be through Sunday announcements, notices in parish publications, support on the church website, and other creative invitations and motivations.

Through the spiritual disciplines of Scripture reading, study, reflection, conversation, and prayer, Threshold Bible Study will help you experience God's grace more abundantly and root your life more deeply in Christ. The risen Jesus said: "Listen! I am standing at the door, knocking; if you hear my voice and open the door, I will come in to you and eat with you, and you with me" (Rev 3:20). Listen to the Word of God, open the door, and cross the threshold to an unimaginable dwelling with God!

SUGGESTIONS FOR INDIVIDUAL STUDY

• Make your Bible reading a time of prayer. Ask for God's guidance as you read the Scriptures.

• Try to study daily, or as often as possible according to the circumstances of your life.

• Read the Bible passage carefully, trying to understand both its meaning and its personal application as you read. Some persons find it helpful to read the passage aloud.

• Read the passage in another Bible translation. Each version adds to your understanding of the original text.

• Allow the commentary to help you comprehend and apply the scriptural text. The commentary is only a beginning, not the last word, on the meaning of the passage.

• After reflecting on each question, write out your responses. The very act of writing will help you clarify your thoughts, bring new insights, and amplify your understanding.

• As you reflect on your answers, think about how you can live God's word in the context of your daily life.

• Conclude each daily lesson by reading the prayer and continuing with your own prayer from the heart.

• Make sure your reflections and prayers are matters of both the mind and the heart. A true encounter with God's word is always a transforming experience.

• Choose a word or a phrase from the lesson to carry with you throughout the day as a reminder of your encounter with God's life-changing word.

• For additional insights and affirmation, share your learning experience with at least one other person whom you trust. The ideal way to share learning is in a small group that meets regularly.

SUGGESTIONS FOR GROUP STUDY

• Meet regularly; weekly is ideal. Try to be on time, and make attendance a high priority for the sake of the group. The average group meets for about an hour.

• Open each session with a prepared prayer, a song, or a reflection. Find some appropriate way to bring the group from the workaday world into a sacred time of graced sharing.

• If you have not been together before, name tags are very helpful as group members begin to become acquainted with one another.

• Spend the first session getting acquainted with one another, reading the Introduction aloud, and discussing the questions that follow.

• Appoint a group facilitator to provide guidance to the discussion. The role of facilitator may rotate among members each week. The facilitator simply keeps the discussion on track; each person shares responsibility for the group. There is no need for the facilitator to be a trained teacher.

• Try to study the six lessons on your own during the week. When you have done your own reflection and written your own answers, you will be better prepared to discuss the six scriptural lessons with the group. If you have not had an opportunity to study the passages during the week, meet with the group anyway to share support and insights.

• Participate in the discussion as much as you are able, offering your thoughts, insights, feelings, and decisions. You learn by sharing with others the fruits of your study.

• Be careful not to dominate the discussion. It is important that everyone in the group be offered an equal opportunity to share the results of their work. Try to link what you say to the comments of others so that the group remains on the topic.

• When discussing your own personal thoughts or feelings, use "I" language. Be as personal and honest as appropriate, and be very cautious about giving advice to others.

• Listen attentively to the other members of the group so as to learn from their insights. The words of the Bible affect each person in a different way, so a group provides a wealth of understanding for each member.

• Don't fear silence. Silence in a group is as important as silence in personal study. It allows individuals time to listen to the voice of God's Spirit and the opportunity to form their thoughts before they speak.

• Solicit several responses for each question. The thoughts of different people will build on the answers of others and will lead to deeper insights for all.

• Don't fear controversy. Differences of opinions are a sign of a healthy and honest group. If you cannot resolve an issue, continue on, agreeing to disagree. There is probably some truth in each viewpoint.

• Discuss the questions that seem most important for the group. There is no need to cover all the questions in the group session.

• Realize that some questions about the Bible cannot be resolved, even by experts. Don't get stuck on some issue for which there are no clear answers.

• Whatever is said in the group is said in confidence and should be regarded as such.

• Pray as a group in whatever way feels comfortable. Pray for the members of your group throughout the week.

Schedule for Group Study

Session 1: Introduction   Date: _1/27/16_

Session 2: Lessons 1–6   Date: _2/3/16_

Session 3: Lessons 7–12   Date: _2/17/16_

Session 4: Lessons 13–18   Date: _2/24_

Session 5: Lessons 19–24   Date: _3/2_

Session 6: Lessons 25–30   Date: _3/9_

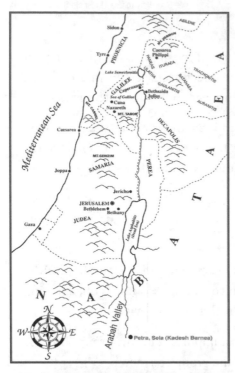

"My eyes have seen your salvation, which you have prepared in the presence of all peoples, a light for revelation to the Gentiles and for glory to your people Israel." Luke 2:30-32

Jesus, the Compassionate Savior (Part 1)

Luke was a gifted writer with an excellent command of the Greek language. He could have chosen any number of forms in which to communicate the good news of Jesus: a letter, like Paul; a homily, like the author of Hebrews; an apocalypse, like John in Revelation. Luke's work is not a catechism or a theological treatise. Rather, Luke chose to write a narrative, "an orderly account of the events" (1:1), a form of literature that many had employed before him.

As a narrative, the gospel of Luke presents the storyline of Jesus' life in order to assure his readers of "the truth concerning the things about which you have been instructed" (1:4). Luke's readers had already been instructed in Christian teaching and the core events of the life of Jesus. But Luke wants to present those events in a way that engages his readers and presents the events of salvation in a grand narrative.

He tells the story not merely as a historical record, but in a way that enables readers to enter the story themselves and to discover it as their own good news. To do this effectively, Luke presents the episodes from the life of Jesus with great detail and concreteness. The narrative uses language that evokes the imagination of the readers and presents episodes from the life of Jesus that become significant within the individual lives of the readers. Luke's artistic description of each scene minimizes his need for long discourses. A brief dialogue or a short saying is enough to engage the readers and communicate the message.

Luke addresses his work to a certain "Theophilus" (1:3), a Gentile man of rank and a recent convert to Christianity. The shape of Luke's gospel suggests that Theophilus was experiencing uncertainty about his place in a movement that was originally Jewish. Yet, Luke did not write just for one person, but for any non-Jew who felt out of place in the church. Theophilus, whose name means "beloved of God," represents all Gentiles seeking to understand God's universal plan of salvation.

Still, after nearly two millennia, Luke's narrative draws in readers who come to experience the story of Jesus as their own. The gospel becomes truly good news for the lives of people today in every nation, of every race, language, and culture. Luke continues to show people how the stories of Jesus transcend their setting in first-century Palestine to speak powerfully to people today.

As we read his narrative, Luke invites us to listen to the word of God and to put it into practice. We can do that by following the example of Mary who reflected on the events of Jesus' life in her heart (2:19, 51). She is the ideal disciple—the one who hears the word of God and observes it (11:28). That is our challenge as we read the narrative of Luke—to become disciples of Jesus by listening, reflecting, and doing the word of God today.

Reflection and discussion

• Why did Luke choose "narrative" as the literary form for communicating the good news of Jesus Christ?

• How can Luke's writings from the ancient world become truly good news for people today?

The Gospel of Salvation for All

Jesus is continually doing the unexpected in Luke's gospel. He upsets people's routine manner of thinking about God's ways and about what salvation means. As we enter the narrative of Luke we should expect to be surprised and even upset at Jesus because he challenges our routine ways of thinking about God. If we are not astounded or disturbed, then we are not reading the gospel afresh. God is the one who casts rulers from their thrones and lifts up the lowly, the one who fills the hungry and empties the rich. When Mary first heard this good news of God's intervention in her life, she was stunned. God wants to intervene in our lives too. Let us expect to be disturbed and changed as we come to experience the story of Jesus as our own.

One of the most obvious characteristics of the writings of Luke is his inclusiveness. All people can come to Jesus and be included in his offer of salvation: the poor and the rich, the Gentiles and the Jews, women and men, foreigners and Israelites, the healthy and the sick, the sinners and the saints. Jesus associates with the sinners, prostitutes, and tax collectors, and he even shares table fellowship with them. The inclusiveness of Jesus' love for all people extends even to those who crucify him, and is demonstrated in his prayer for their forgiveness. Our call to evangelize is rooted in the mission he gave his church to extend his salvation to all people.

The gospel presents a new way of relating to God by turning to him through Jesus. This plan of God for salvation includes peoples of all ethnicities and backgrounds. The mission of Jesus is stated in several forms: he came "to bring good news to the poor" (4:18), "to call not the righteous but sinners to repentance" (5:32), "to seek out and to save the lost" (19:10). Luke shows that all who are needy can encounter a concerned and compassionate God through Jesus. As Savior, Messiah, and Lord (2:11), Jesus is the divine instrument of God's plan to save the world. His message is one of hope and transformation. God's promises, revealed in the ancient Scriptures, are fulfilled for all who turn to Jesus, reorient their lives, and trust in him. This salvation involves sharing in hope, receiving forgiveness, experiencing God's kingdom, and being enlivened by the Holy Spirit. Such care and compassion know no boundaries of race, gender, or class.

Luke's gospel should be read within the context of Luke's two-volume work: the Gospel according to Luke and the Acts of the Apostles. Acts is a continuation of the narrative of the gospel. It begins when Jesus is taken up into heaven, and it tells the story of the early church. Volume one is the gospel of Jesus Christ; volume two may be called the good news of the Holy Spirit. The two volumes form one continuous narrative, showing the spread of God's salvation from ancient Israel to all the nations of the earth. Luke writes his gospel in a way that demonstrates how the ministry of Jesus relates to the life of the early church and how being disciples of Jesus means belonging to the people who continue to follow him as the resurrected Savior and universal Lord.

Reflection and discussion

• What does it mean to me to acknowledge Jesus as the Savior?

• What might be an important message that Luke's gospel could offer to people in our culture today?

Prayer Is the Heart of Luke's Gospel

Luke's writing is filled with a spirit of prayer. This prayerful tone is conveyed to us in several ways in his gospel. First, the gospel contains four prayers that have become the most exalted prayers of the church through the ages. Second, Luke shows Jesus at prayer more than any other evangelist. Jesus prays often during his public life and demonstrates that regular prayer is essential for anyone who wants to follow in his way. Third, Luke shows Jesus teaching his disciples to pray and includes several teachings and parables about prayer that are found only in his gospel.

The four prayers from Luke's gospel come to us on the lips of four prayerful people whose examples teach us to pray: Zechariah, Mary, Simeon, and Jesus. These four prayers have been incorporated in the liturgical prayer of the church. The church's morning prayer culminates in the prayer of Zechariah: "Blessed be the Lord God of Israel..." (Luke 1:68-79). The evening liturgical prayer leads up to the prayer of Mary: "My soul magnifies the Lord, and my spirit rejoices in God my Savior..." (1:46-55). Both of these hours of prayer conclude with the prayer that Jesus taught, the prayer that is included in the Communion rite of every Eucharistic liturgy, his prayer to the Father (11:2-4). Finally, the night prayer of the church features the prayer of Simeon: "Master, now you are dismissing your servant in peace, according to your word..." (2:29-32).

Throughout his gospel, Luke continually makes special note of the fact that Jesus prayed. These times in which Jesus is described as being at prayer are mostly moments of revelation, decision, and transition in the gospel. Luke is the only gospel to state that Jesus was praying after his baptism (3:21). His prayer continues through the descent of the Holy Spirit and the voice of God from heaven declaring Jesus his beloved Son. This critical moment at the inauguration of Jesus' public life takes place within the context of Jesus' prayerful communication with the Father.

Like the revelation of Jesus at his baptism, his revelation at the scene of transfiguration also takes place in the context of prayerful communion with God. Jesus "went up on the mountain to pray" and the appearance of Jesus was transfigured "while he was praying" (9:28-29). At both the baptism and transfiguration of Jesus, Luke tells his readers that prayer must be the setting in which we discover and discern the significance of Jesus for our lives.

Luke is careful to note that Jesus demonstrated a balance between his public ministry and his life of solitary prayer. He reports that great crowds assembled to listen to the teaching of Jesus and to be cured of illnesses. However, Luke says, Jesus "would withdraw to deserted places and pray" (5:16). The tense of the Greek verb here suggests that the withdrawal of Jesus for prayer was a repeated action. Jesus would periodically withdraw for the purpose of prayer during his busy public life.

Luke tells us that Jesus, before choosing the twelve apostles, "went out to the mountain to pray; and he spent the night in prayer to God" (6:12). His praying on the mountain throughout the night enabled him to make that critical choice wisely and confidently. Another critical moment of the gospel occurs when Jesus questions his disciples concerning his identity: "Who do the crowds say that I am? Who do you say that I am?" Only Luke sets this crucial scene in the context of prayer: "Once when Jesus was praying alone, with only the disciples near him" (9:18). Jesus could have been praying privately while his disciples were around him, or Jesus could have been praying with his disciples but away from the crowds. Either way, the scene teaches us that discerning the identity of Jesus and who he is in our lives is done best in quiet, reflective prayer.

Finally, Luke shows us that prayer was the context in which Jesus began and ended his passion. At the Last Supper Jesus tells Peter, "I have prayed for you that your own faith may not fail" (22:32), as he foretells Peter's denial and repentance. When Jesus went to the Mount of Olives before his arrest, Luke notes that he went to a particular place where he prayed regularly. There Jesus asked his closest disciples to pray. And he withdrew from them a ways and then knelt down to pray intensely to his Father (22:39-41). Jesus prays in agony, asking that the cup of suffering pass from him, but also surrendering himself to the Father's will. At the end of his passion, the final words of Jesus are from Israel's book of prayer, the Psalms. "Father, into your hands I commend my spirit" (23:46; Psalm 31:5) is the prayer of Jesus from the cross as he breathed his last.

The disciples must have seen Jesus go away often for times of prayer. They saw how important prayer was for Jesus, and they saw how Jesus prayed in all the critical moments of his life. Jesus gave silent witness to the value of prayer, and it was this personal witness that inspired his disciples to request that he teach them to pray. Luke tells us that Jesus "was praying in a certain place, and after he had finished, one of his disciples said to him, 'Lord, teach us to pray'"

(11:1). Luke invites us, his readers, to go off with Jesus and to learn from him how to pray.

Jesus taught his disciples to pray as he prayed (11:2-4). The prayer is addressed to God as Father, showing disciples that we can share in Jesus' intimate relationship with God. It is simple and direct; it praises God, requests the basic needs of life, and asks for God's forgiveness. It is the prayer the Christian community has continued to pray since the days of Jesus.

The Lord's Prayer in Luke is followed by teachings of Jesus about prayer. Jesus exhorts his disciples to be persistent in prayer by telling of a man who came to a friend in the middle of the night to borrow bread for a traveler to whom he was offering hospitality. Though the friend did not get up immediately, he eventually got up to "give him whatever he needs" because of the man's persistence in asking (11:5-8). Jesus teaches persistence in prayer not because we have to convince God to answer us or to wear down God's resistance. Jesus teaches persistence, rather, to overcome our tendency to give up on prayer too easily or to pray too sporadically.

Jesus then urges the disciples to pray with confidence. Though we may sometimes wonder whether our prayers are heard by God, Jesus declares, "Ask, and it will be given to you; search, and you will find; knock, and the door will be opened for you" (11:9). He compares the generosity of an earthly father with the lavish generosity of God. Jesus concludes this teaching by asking, "If you then…know how to give good gifts to your children, how much more will the heavenly Father give the Holy Spirit to those who ask him!" (11:13). We can have the utmost confidence because God is more than a friend; God is a loving Father who knows and responds to all our needs.

In another section of the gospel, Jesus teaches about prayer by telling two parables. The point of the first parable is provided by Luke's introduction: "Jesus told them a parable about their need to pray always and not to lose heart" (18:1). In the parable a widow continues to insist on her rights from a corrupt and dishonest judge. Because of her persistence, the judge rendered a favorable decision for her (18:2-5). "Will not God then secure the rights of his chosen ones who call out to him day and night?" (18:7), Jesus asks. We might not think that God is hearing our prayer; we might get discouraged and quit praying when we do not seem to get results. But we ought never to lose heart; we can trust in God to answer our prayers.

The second parable tells of a Pharisee and a tax collector who both went up to the temple to pray. The Pharisee told God all that he was doing and bragged about his "spiritual" accomplishments (18:11-12). The tax collector, in contrast, beat his breast and offered a simple and humble prayer: "God, be merciful to me, a sinner!" (18:13). The parable teaches us to express our dependence on God's mercy, aware of our need of forgiveness and grace.

Jesus' final teaching on prayer comes as he enters his passion and is praying on the Mount of Olives. He told his disciples, "Get up and pray that you may not come into the time of trial" (22:46). As Jesus was experiencing his prayerful agony, he was teaching his disciples to pray in times of tribulation and turmoil. As Jesus demonstrates, prayer can be an act of desperation in the critical moments of life. It can be what we do when we don't know what else can be done.

In all of these ways, Luke shows that prayer is the heart of the gospel. By showing his disciples how to pray, when to pray, and why to pray, Jesus encourages them to be a prayerful community. These teachings of Jesus take root in the disciples, and so the Acts of the Apostles demonstrates that prayer is at the heart of the early church. The community of disciples takes the teachings of Jesus to heart and prays, not only at times of decision and transition in the church, but as part of the regular rhythm of Christian life. In this way, Luke's gospel continually forms each generation of disciples into a community of prayer.

Reflection and discussion

• What are the moments in the life of Jesus in which Luke spotlights the prayer of Jesus?

• How does the example of Jesus' prayer in the gospel encourage and inspire my own life of prayer?

Learning to Read Luke's Good News

There is a tradition retained in Greek Orthodox Christianity that Luke was a painter. Whether or not there is any historical validity to this understanding, we can imagine Luke painting many of the scenes that he so vividly describes in his gospel. If he didn't paint with oils, we know that he certainly painted with words. And the beautiful images he gives us in his gospel have inspired artists through the centuries of Christianity to present his gospel stories in frescoes, mosaics, icons, stained glass, and canvas.

Learning how to appreciate a work of art can also teach us about how to approach the Scriptures. Sometimes we read the Bible with too much emphasis on simply learning information, on understanding what the text says. Understanding the Scriptures does not necessarily mean being able to interpret every sentence on every page. Sometimes what we need to do is simply reflect in wonder on the images presented in the sacred text and notice the emotions that arise in our hearts. This seems to be what Mary did. She had a contemplative sense of wonder toward these divine mysteries. She kept all of these things and pondered them in her heart. We can learn from Mary how to reflectively ponder the good news of her Son as a work of art.

A second ancient tradition claims that Luke was a physician. In fact, Paul refers to Luke in his letter to the Colossians as "the beloved physician" (Col 4:14). Whether or not Luke practiced as a medical doctor, we can be sure that Luke was a person very sensitive to people in need. His gospel reflects more than any other gospel the human needs of the poor, ill, and suffering. Perhaps this description of Luke can help us learn to read the gospel with another emphasis. When Luke describes scenes of people who are ill or cast aside, he is encouraging us to look for similar scenes in our own world, and then to do something about them. The gospel of Luke invites us to be instruments in the healing of others in order to be disciples in our own world today. Like Mary, we can become active contemplatives, "those who hear the word of God and do it" (8:21).

Finally, Luke is known in the Christian tradition as a companion of Paul. In his letter to Philemon, Paul mentions Luke as one of his "fellow workers" (Phlm 24). In recounting Paul's travels in the Acts of the Apostles, Luke often uses the pronoun "we." These so-called "we" sections portray the author as a traveling companion of Paul. With the great "apostle to the Gentiles," Luke learned to evangelize, to proclaim the gospel in word and in deed, with passion and with love. Contemplating his gospel can help us, too, be ardent disciples, devoted to helping others know and understand the good news of Jesus Christ as God's plan for the world's salvation.

Reflection and discussion

• How can I better appreciate the gospel by understanding Luke's work as that of a literary artist?

• What am I hoping to experience as I begin to study and reflect on this Gospel according to Luke?

Prayer

Lord God, you raised up Luke among the peoples of the Gentile world to receive the gospel of Jesus Christ and to evangelize through writing this narrative of his life. Prepare my heart to encounter Jesus through the pages of this Gospel according to Luke. Stir up within me a deep desire to know and follow him more deeply and personally. Show me how to take these words to heart and to meditate upon them. Help me to respond to the invitation of Jesus to listen, reflect, and do the word of God today. Keep me faithful these weeks to the challenges of study and prayer that your word offers to me.

SUGGESTIONS FOR FACILITATORS, GROUP SESSION 1

1. If the group is meeting for the first time, or if there are newcomers joining the group, it is helpful to provide nametags.

2. Distribute the books to the members of the group.

3. You may want to ask the participants to introduce themselves and tell the group a bit about themselves.

4. Ask one or more of these introductory questions:
   • What drew you to join this group?
   • What is your biggest fear in beginning this Bible study?
   • How is beginning this study like a "threshold" for you?

5. You may want to pray this prayer as a group:

   Come upon us, Holy Spirit, to enlighten and guide us as we begin this study of Luke's gospel. You inspired the writers of the Scriptures to reveal your presence throughout the history of salvation. This inspired word has the power to convert our hearts and change our lives. Fill our hearts with desire, trust, and confidence as you shine the light of your truth within us. Motivate us to read the Scriptures, and give us a deeper love for God's word each day. Bless us during this session and throughout the coming week with the fire of your love.

6. Read the Introduction aloud, pausing at each question for discussion. Group members may wish to write the insights of the group as each question is discussed. Encourage several members of the group to respond to each question.

7. Don't feel compelled to finish the complete Introduction during the session. It is better to allow sufficient time to talk about the questions raised than to rush to the end. Group members may read any remaining sections on their own after the group meeting.

8. Instruct group members to read the first six lessons on their own during the six days before the next group meeting. They should write out their own answers to the questions as preparation for next week's group discussion.

9. Fill in the date for each group meeting under "Schedule for Group Study."

10. Conclude the session by praying aloud together the prayer at the end of the Introduction.

"With the spirit and power of Elijah he will go before him,
to turn the hearts of parents to their children,
and the disobedient to the wisdom of the righteous,
to make ready a people prepared for the Lord." Luke 1:17

Preparing God's People for Salvation

LUKE 1:1-25 ¹*Since many have undertaken to set down an orderly account of the events that have been fulfilled among us, ²just as they were handed on to us by those who from the beginning were eyewitnesses and servants of the word, ³I too decided, after investigating everything carefully from the very first, to write an orderly account for you, most excellent Theophilus, ⁴so that you may know the truth concerning the things about which you have been instructed.*

⁵In the days of King Herod of Judea, there was a priest named Zechariah, who belonged to the priestly order of Abijah. His wife was a descendant of Aaron, and her name was Elizabeth. ⁶Both of them were righteous before God, living blamelessly according to all the commandments and regulations of the Lord. ⁷But they had no children, because Elizabeth was barren, and both were getting on in years.

⁸Once when he was serving as priest before God and his section was on duty, ⁹he was chosen by lot, according to the custom of the priesthood, to enter the sanctuary of the Lord and offer incense. ¹⁰Now at the time of the incense offering, the whole assembly of the people was praying outside. ¹¹Then there appeared

to him an angel of the Lord, standing at the right side of the altar of incense.
[12] *When Zechariah saw him, he was terrified; and fear overwhelmed him.* [13] *But the angel said to him, "Do not be afraid, Zechariah, for your prayer has been heard. Your wife Elizabeth will bear you a son, and you will name him John.* [14] *You will have joy and gladness, and many will rejoice at his birth,* [15] *for he will be great in the sight of the Lord. He must never drink wine or strong drink; even before his birth he will be filled with the Holy Spirit.* [16] *He will turn many of the people of Israel to the Lord their God.* [17] *With the spirit and power of Elijah he will go before him, to turn the hearts of parents to their children, and the disobedient to the wisdom of the righteous, to make ready a people prepared for the Lord."* [18] *Zechariah said to the angel, "How will I know that this is so? For I am an old man, and my wife is getting on in years."* [19] *The angel replied, "I am Gabriel. I stand in the presence of God, and I have been sent to speak to you and to bring you this good news.* [20] *But now, because you did not believe my words, which will be fulfilled in their time, you will become mute, unable to speak, until the day these things occur."*

[21] *Meanwhile the people were waiting for Zechariah, and wondered at his delay in the sanctuary.* [22] *When he did come out, he could not speak to them, and they realized that he had seen a vision in the sanctuary. He kept motioning to them and remained unable to speak.* [23] *When his time of service was ended, he went to his home.*

[24] *After those days his wife Elizabeth conceived, and for five months she remained in seclusion. She said,* [25] *"This is what the Lord has done for me when he looked favorably on me and took away the disgrace I have endured among my people."*

The preface to the gospel indicates that Luke wrote to offer an accurate history of the events associated with Jesus Christ. He refers to earlier written accounts (verse 1), to eyewitnesses who preach God's word (verse 2), and to a careful investigation and an orderly sequence (verse 3). These elements of his writing all contribute to a narrative that assures Theophilus and all of Luke's readers of the truth concerning God's saving plan, which came to its fullness in Jesus (verse 4).

Because Luke is not himself one of the apostolic witnesses, but rather a second-generation Christian, he relies on the apostolic tradition that came before him for his narrative. This tradition includes the other gospels and Christian texts that were written prior to this one as well as the eyewitness testimony that Luke received from others. He has to carefully investigate these events since he did not experience them himself. Luke feels that he has something to contribute to this tradition with his own gospel, and this preface places his work alongside other writings about Jesus and his church. He offers a fresh presentation of salvation history, beginning with the birth of John the Baptist and continuing, at the end of Acts, to the extension of the church into Rome.

Luke's infancy accounts plunge us into the world of ancient Israel, with its Torah, temple, and priesthood. Zechariah is a priest offering incense in the temple, and Elizabeth is elderly and childless, like Sarah and other women of ancient Israel (verses 5-7). Elizabeth and Zechariah follow the law of the covenant and are ideal Jews. By way of all these allusions to the Hebrew Scriptures, Luke demonstrates that the coming of Jesus into the world is rooted in the historical faith of Israel.

The incense offering coincided with the twice-daily sacrifice at the temple and with the offering of morning and evening prayer. Zechariah enters the temple's inner sanctuary, the Holy Place, to offer the incense, a symbol of intercession proceeding up to God on behalf of the people. At this solemn moment of prayer, God acts for his people in sending his angelic messenger to Zechariah. Gabriel announces the good news of John's birth with words of comfort.

The announcement indicates a theme that Luke will develop throughout his gospel: God answers prayers in ways that far surpass human expectations (verses 13, 25). Zechariah and Elizabeth, as well as all the people of Israel, have prayed and waited for the announcement made that day in the temple. The long history of waiting is about to end, and the prayers of God's people are about to be answered. The result is "joy and gladness" for Zechariah and rejoicing by many in Israel (verse 14), for this birth means that salvation is drawing near.

The child's name, John, means "Yahweh has shown favor." Through John's ministry, God will begin the work of salvation in a way that reverses and exceeds the expectations of all. The angel describes John's character and ministry. He will be "great in the sight of the Lord" because he will live to serve God (verse 15). His lifestyle will be one of personal discipline, living the asceticism of a prophet, and he will be "filled with the Holy Spirit." As the last of

Israel's great prophets, he will return many to their covenant with God and will "make ready a people prepared for the Lord" (verse 17). As a transitional figure in God's saving plan, he represents a bridge between promise and fulfillment.

Filled with uncertainty and needing support for his faith, Zechariah asks for a sign. In response, Gabriel tells him that he will be unable to speak until the things he has announced have come to pass (verses 18-20). Zechariah's muteness will teach him a lesson in trust, and it will also have the effect of concealing the revelation from the crowd until the proper time and building up a mood of anticipation within the narrative.

Reflection and discussion

• Why is Luke so concerned to demonstrate that Zechariah and Elizabeth are devoted Jews, faithfully living Israel's covenant with God?

• The Bible demonstrates some prayerful requests answered immediately, others answered eventually, and still others denied for a better way. What might be God's intention in granting the prayers of Zechariah and Elizabeth only when their request seemed impossible?

Prayer

Lord God, as I begin to study your good news, you desire to bring good news to my life as you conveyed it to your ancient people. Give me a spirit of joy and gladness as I receive your word. Help me to look for unexpected messages and to anticipate the new ways you wish to work in my life.

"Surely, from now on all generations will call me blessed;
for the Mighty One has done great things for me,
and holy is his name." Luke 1:48-49

Mary is Pregnant with Child and with Hope

LUKE 1:26-56 ²⁶*In the sixth month the angel Gabriel was sent by God to a town in Galilee called Nazareth,* ²⁷*to a virgin engaged to a man whose name was Joseph, of the house of David. The virgin's name was Mary.* ²⁸*And he came to her and said, "Greetings, favored one! The Lord is with you."* ²⁹*But she was much perplexed by his words and pondered what sort of greeting this might be.* ³⁰*The angel said to her, "Do not be afraid, Mary, for you have found favor with God.* ³¹*And now, you will conceive in your womb and bear a son, and you will name him Jesus.* ³²*He will be great, and will be called the Son of the Most High, and the Lord God will give to him the throne of his ancestor David.* ³³*He will reign over the house of Jacob forever, and of his kingdom there will be no end."* ³⁴*Mary said to the angel, "How can this be, since I am a virgin?"* ³⁵*The angel said to her, "The Holy Spirit will come upon you, and the power of the Most High will over-shadow you; therefore the child to be born will be holy; he will be called Son of God.* ³⁶*And now, your relative Elizabeth in her old age has also conceived a son; and this is the sixth month for her who was said to be barren.* ³⁷*For nothing will be impossible with God."* ³⁸*Then Mary said, "Here am I, the servant of the Lord; let it be with me according to your word." Then the angel departed from her.*

³⁹*In those days Mary set out and went with haste to a Judean town in the hill country,* ⁴⁰*where she entered the house of Zechariah and greeted Elizabeth.* ⁴¹*When Elizabeth heard Mary's greeting, the child leaped in her womb. And Elizabeth was filled with the Holy Spirit* ⁴²*and exclaimed with a loud cry, "Blessed are you among women, and blessed is the fruit of your womb.* ⁴³*And why has this happened to me, that the mother of my Lord comes to me?* ⁴⁴*For as soon as I heard the sound of your greeting, the child in my womb leaped for joy.* ⁴⁵*And blessed is she who believed that there would be a fulfillment of what was spoken to her by the Lord."*

⁴⁶*And Mary said,*

"My soul magnifies the Lord,

⁴⁷*and my spirit rejoices in God my Savior,*

⁴⁸*for he has looked with favor on the lowliness of his servant.*

Surely, from now on all generations will call me blessed;

⁴⁹*for the Mighty One has done great things for me,*

and holy is his name.

⁵⁰*His mercy is for those who fear him*

from generation to generation.

⁵¹*He has shown strength with his arm;*

he has scattered the proud in the thoughts of their hearts.

⁵²*He has brought down the powerful from their thrones,*

and lifted up the lowly;

⁵³*he has filled the hungry with good things,*

and sent the rich away empty.

⁵⁴*He has helped his servant Israel,*

in remembrance of his mercy,

⁵⁵*according to the promise he made to our ancestors,*

to Abraham and to his descendants forever."

⁵⁶*And Mary remained with her about three months and then returned to her home.*

L uke patterns this birth announcement scene on similar announce- ments in the Old Testament (see Judges 13:2-7), and he creates a parallel to the announcement to Zechariah. The two annunciations are like a diptych, a painting consisting of two panels hinged together. Gabriel appears in both scenes, telling Zechariah and Mary not to be afraid (verses 13, 30) and announcing the unexpected birth of their children (verses 13, 31). Both are reassured after raising an objection (verses 18-19, 34-35), and a sign is given to each (verses 20, 36).

Yet, there are stark contrasts between the two scenes. The announcement about John comes to a priest in the midst of public worship at the temple, while the announcement about Jesus comes privately to a humble woman in a small village. The simplicity of this annunciation matches the tone of Jesus' ministry. Furthermore, Elizabeth is elderly and barren, while Mary is youthful and virgin. Elizabeth conceives a child in her old age, like other women of ancient Israel. The conception of Jesus is unlike anything before in salvation history. The story emphasizes twice in verse 27 that Mary is a virgin; in verse 34 it further confirms this lack of sexual experience. God's intervention in her life was not the result of anything she could have anticipated.

As Gabriel greets Mary, he declares her to be the one who has been favored with the unmerited grace of God. Her son will be the Messiah, the one who will receive the throne of his ancestor, King David, and his reign will be ever-lasting, fulfilling the promises of the ancient covenant (verses 32-33). He will also be the Son of God, conceived through the overshadowing power of God's Spirit. "The Most High," "the Son of God," and "the Holy Spirit," described as the Trinity in later doctrine, are present here at this climactic moment of amazing grace (verse 35). Mary responds with perfect humility, "Let it be with me according to your word" (verse 38), and as obediently as her son will respond to God's will in the garden before his death, "Not my will but yours be done" (22:42). Mary stands in the middle of this drama as God's listening, humble, and willing servant. She receives the word of God in her heart, and consents to conceive the Son of God in her womb. Mary's assent is totally free and not made without considering its costly consequences. Yet Mary proclaims herself the Lord's servant and states: whatever it costs, wherever it takes me, I will do it.

Mary's travel from Nazareth to "a Judean town in the hill country" is a long and arduous journey. But Mary goes without hesitation to visit her kins-woman Elizabeth, whom she knows is also miraculously pregnant. In the scene of their visit, the two annunciation accounts, of John and of Jesus, are brought together. In this encounter, the elderly Elizabeth represents God's work among the people of ancient Israel; Mary represents the new work that

God will do in the sending of the Messiah. In Elizabeth, the old esteems the new; in Mary, the new honors the old. As a model of Christian discipleship, Mary, after receiving the good news, hastens to share it with another.

Mary's song demonstrates that she is the representative of God's people. The mercy shown to her reflects the mercy that God has shown to Israel (verses 49, 54) and is a response to the promises God had made long ago (verse 55). The song proclaims that Mary's state of lowliness has been unexpectedly reversed, so that now "all generations will call me blessed" (verse 48). Likewise, God reverses all that people have come to expect: he disperses the arrogant, throws down the rulers, and sends the rich away empty. But God also lifts up the lowly, fills the hungry, and helps Israel (verses 51-54). In this encounter, God is named as Lord (verse 46), Savior (verse 47), and holy (verse 49). Jesus has already been called holy (verse 35); he is praised as Lord (verse 43); and he will be called Savior (2:11).

Since the word of God permeated the heart of Mary, she would have been quite familiar with the passages from the Scriptures of Israel that echo throughout her canticle. Mary is part of a long line of women who sing songs of praise in the Old Testament: Miriam (Exod 15:20-21), Deborah (Judg 5), Hannah (1 Sam 2:1-10), and Judith (Jdt 16:1-17). The canticle is also modeled on the Psalms, the daily hymns of the Jewish people. Mary sings back to God the truths that she learned in her daily reflection on the word of God. Her canticle rings with pure praise of God. Mary is a model of living faith because she recognized what God was doing through her, she accepted it joyfully, and she was humble enough to give God all the glory.

Reflection and discussion

• Mary was powerless is a world in which power ruled, young in a society that valued age, poor in a culture divided into classes, and female in a world ruled by men. In what sense is she God's perfect instrument for bringing salvation to the world?

• The annunciations to Zechariah and to Mary show similarities and contrasts. How do these parallels demonstrate that God is doing something new and unexpected in the coming of Jesus?

• How does Mary's song describe the qualities of the coming reign of Christ?

• What are some emotions that Mary must have felt throughout the Annunciation and the Visitation?

Prayer

Mighty Lord, you have done great things for me and for all your people. Thank you for continuing to fulfill your promises to me, and help me to be grateful for all you have done. Holy God, you chose Mary to be the mother of your Son. Help me to be as willing to listen to you and as obedient to do your will as Mary.

"By the tender mercy of our God, the dawn from on high will break upon us, to give light to those who sit in darkness and in the shadow of death."
Luke 1:78-79

The Breaking Dawn Illumines the Darkness

LUKE 1:57-80 *57Now the time came for Elizabeth to give birth, and she bore a son. 58Her neighbors and relatives heard that the Lord had shown his great mercy to her, and they rejoiced with her.*

59On the eighth day they came to circumcise the child, and they were going to name him Zechariah after his father. 60But his mother said, "No; he is to be called John." 61They said to her, "None of your relatives has this name." 62Then they began motioning to his father to find out what name he wanted to give him. 63He asked for a writing tablet and wrote, "His name is John." And all of them were amazed. 64Immediately his mouth was opened and his tongue freed, and he began to speak, praising God. 65Fear came over all their neighbors, and all these things were talked about throughout the entire hill country of Judea. 66All who heard them pondered them and said, "What then will this child become?" For, indeed, the hand of the Lord was with him.

67Then his father Zechariah was filled with the Holy Spirit and spoke this prophecy:

68"Blessed be the Lord God of Israel,
  for he has looked favorably on his people and redeemed them.

⁶⁹*He has raised up a mighty savior for us*
  in the house of his servant David,
⁷⁰*as he spoke through the mouth of his holy prophets from of old,*
  ⁷¹*that we would be saved from our enemies*
  and from the hand of all who hate us.
⁷²*Thus he has shown the mercy promised to our ancestors,*
  and has remembered his holy covenant,
⁷³*the oath that he swore to our ancestor Abraham,*
  to grant us ⁷⁴*that we, being rescued from the hands of our enemies,*
might serve him without fear, ⁷⁵*in holiness and righteousness*
  before him all our days.
⁷⁶*And you, child, will be called the prophet of the Most High;*
  for you will go before the Lord to prepare his ways,
⁷⁷*to give knowledge of salvation to his people*
  by the forgiveness of their sins.
⁷⁸*By the tender mercy of our God,*
  the dawn from on high will break upon us,
⁷⁹*to give light to those who sit in darkness and in the shadow of death,*
  to guide our feet into the way of peace."
⁸⁰*The child grew and became strong in spirit, and he was in the wilderness*
  until the day he appeared publicly to Israel.

The angel's announcement, that Elizabeth will bear a son and that many will rejoice at his birth, comes to fulfillment. God shows his great mercy to her, and all rejoice with her. John's parents are careful to observe the law that states that their child must be circumcised on the eighth day following his birth. Reversing the social expectation that the child would be named after his father, Zechariah and Elizabeth insist that their child be named John (verses 60, 63). When Zechariah writes "John is his name," he is immediately liberated from his muteness and freed to speak. He praises God and begins to prophesy. God's will is done despite expectations to the contrary, and Zechariah has learned to trust God's word even more.

The birth of John, the unusual name given to the child, and the return of Zechariah's speech lead to a sense of fear among the people, knowing that God is powerfully at work among them. The events also lead the people to ponder and discuss these occurrences. The question, "What then will this child become?" raises a sense of expectation about the role that John will have in God's plan and sets the scene for Zechariah's prophetic song.

Zechariah's hymn of praise serves as inspired commentary on the events surrounding the birth of John. Zechariah is convinced that God's plan of salvation is moving to its completion with these new divine actions. Zechariah praises "the Lord God of Israel" (verse 68) who has shown mercy to their ancestors and remembered "his holy covenant" (verse 72). He extols God for fulfilling the oath he made with Abraham (verse 73) and for raising up a Messiah within the house of David (verse 69). The hymn specifies that, through the prophetic work of John and the coming of the Messiah, the God of Israel is redeeming his people.

With Zechariah "freed" to praise God, he proclaims the freedom that God brings about for his people. God's people are rescued from the hands of enemies and liberated to worship God (verse 74). Here is a new "exodus" for the nation. God saves his people for service so that they might serve him fearlessly "in holiness and righteousness." The essence of this service is responsiveness to God's will, a worship that is personal and moral and that spans the lifetimes of God's faithful ones.

The role of John as "the prophet of the Most High" is to prepare the way for God, who will come to his people through the Messiah, Jesus. John heralds the arrival of God's salvation, and his message centers on "the forgiveness of sins" (verse 77). As Luke develops the figure of John, he associates this forerunner with the message of salvation, the forgiveness of sins, and the baptism of repentance.

In contrast to John, the role of the Messiah, as "the dawn" that comes from God, is to scatter the darkness of sin and death and guide God's people "into the way of peace" (verses 78-79). The Messiah's light refers to his coming to humanity, his teaching God's way, and his ministering salvation. All of these messianic works are the concrete expressions of God's compassion, his "tender mercy." As the bright morning star or the rising sun, Jesus brings salvation by showing God's people "the way" that leads to a complete and harmonious relationship with God. Instruction in this "way" of Jesus is the mission of the remainder of Luke's writing.

Reflection and discussion

• What seems to be God's purpose in making Zechariah unable to speak until the naming of John? What occurs within Zechariah during this period of muteness?

• In what ways does the prophecy of Zechariah describe the redemption God brings to Israel as an "exodus"?

• Zechariah shows that faith comes slowly for some. How can I emulate the faith he manifested in his song of praise?

Prayer

God of Israel, you brought redemption to your chosen people after a long time of waiting. Help me to be faithful to your new covenant, to live as your child in freedom, and to worship you in holiness.

The angel said to them, "Do not be afraid; for see—
I am bringing you good news of great joy for all the people:
to you is born this day in the city of David a Savior,
who is the Messiah, the Lord." Luke 2:10-11

Birth of the Savior, Messiah, and Lord

LUKE 2:1-21 *¹In those days a decree went out from Emperor Augustus that all the world should be registered. ²This was the first registration and was taken while Quirinius was governor of Syria. ³All went to their own towns to be registered. ⁴Joseph also went from the town of Nazareth in Galilee to Judea, to the city of David called Bethlehem, because he was descended from the house and family of David. ⁵He went to be registered with Mary, to whom he was engaged and who was expecting a child. ⁶While they were there, the time came for her to deliver her child. ⁷And she gave birth to her firstborn son and wrapped him in bands of cloth, and laid him in a manger, because there was no place for them in the inn.*

⁸In that region there were shepherds living in the fields, keeping watch over their flock by night. ⁹Then an angel of the Lord stood before them, and the glory of the Lord shone around them, and they were terrified. ¹⁰But the angel said to them, "Do not be afraid; for see—I am bringing you good news of great joy for all the people: ¹¹to you is born this day in the city of David a Savior, who is the Messiah, the Lord. ¹²This will be a sign for you: you will find a child wrapped in bands of cloth and lying in a manger." [13] *And suddenly there was with the angel a multitude of the heavenly host, praising God and saying,*

[14] *"Glory to God in the highest heaven,*
    and on earth peace among those whom he favors!"

[15] *When the angels had left them and gone into heaven, the shepherds said to one another, "Let us go now to Bethlehem and see this thing that has taken place, which the Lord has made known to us."* [16] *So they went with haste and found Mary and Joseph, and the child lying in the manger.* [17] *When they saw this, they made known what had been told them about this child;* [18] *and all who heard it were amazed at what the shepherds told them.* [19] *But Mary treasured all these words and pondered them in her heart.* [20] *The shepherds returned, glorifying and praising God for all they had heard and seen, as it had been told them.*

[21] *After eight days had passed, it was time to circumcise the child; and he was called Jesus, the name given by the angel before he was conceived in the womb.*

From the simple Jewish setting in Nazareth, the lives of Mary and Joseph enter a drama that connects them to the Roman Empire and indeed "all the world" (verse 1). While Joseph and Mary travel to Bethlehem, the whole world is also on the move. The appearance of the angel and the heavenly message connect this drama not only with the earth but with heaven as well (verses 9-13).

Jesus is born in the Jewish town of Bethlehem, but that little village has become the focus of heaven and earth. The child to be born there is both the "Messiah" of Israel and the "Lord" of heaven and earth (verse 11); he is Son of David (verse 4) as well as Son of God. The angels give glory to God who reigns in heaven, and they evoke peace for the people of the earth (verse 14).

The details of Jesus' birth are humble and simple. Giving birth in first-century Palestine would have been like giving birth in some war-ravaged area of our world today. Emperors and their armies oppressed the people; corruption and extortion were a way of life. The Bible doesn't say how Mary and Joseph reached Bethlehem from Nazareth, but traveling on foot was the usual means of travel for the poor. On donkey or on foot, the journey would have been exhausting.

Joseph and Mary are travelers, lacking adequate shelter. Our Christmas cards have painted the stable with glowing softness, but if tradition is correct,

Jesus was born in one of the many caves that perforate the hills around Bethlehem. The conditions were probably rather dreadful, more like giving birth in some abandoned hovel of an urban alleyway today. Mary wrapped her newborn in cloth strips, as was the custom, and placed him in a manger, a feeding trough for animals. As Luke shows so consistently, God works in ways that seem unlikely and unexpected.

The description of Jesus as Mary's "firstborn son" (verse 7) is not intended to refer to the size of Mary's family and does not indicate that Mary must have had other children. Rather, the term designates that Jesus was to have the status associated with the firstborn according to the Torah: consecrated to God (Exod 13:2; Num 3:13) and receiving the father's inheritance (Deut 21:17).

The firstborn of Mary is also proclaimed in the New Testament as the firstborn of God, just as Israel and the Davidic king were proclaimed God's firstborn in the Old Testament. Jesus is the "firstborn of all creation" (Col 1:15) and God's firstborn in the world (Heb 1:6). The future children of Mary will be all those who follow Jesus since he is the "firstborn within a large family" (Rom 8:29).

The shepherds in the fields are among the lowliest laborers of the land. Yet, the one announced to them by the angels is "a Savior, who is the Messiah, the Lord" (verse 11). These three titles of Jesus—Savior, Messiah, and Lord—describe the mission of Jesus as it is developed throughout Luke's writings.

"Savior" points to his role as the one who delivers God's people. "Messiah" designates his regal office as the promised Anointed One of God. "Lord" indicates his sovereign authority. Although Jesus is born under the reign of Caesar Augustus, whose titles are just as majestic, for Luke the key historical figure is not the Roman emperor but the frail child Jesus, the royal Savior and Lord of all.

Luke's gospel portrays Jesus at the beginning and end of the gospel in a most unusual way: he is born in a stable for animals and will die on a cross with criminals. The "sign" of Luke's gospel given to the shepherds also points to the gospel's close. The child "wrapped in bands of cloth and lying in a manger" (verse 12) anticipates the crucified one who will be "wrapped in a linen cloth and laid in a rock-hewn tomb" (23:53). This connection between the newborn Savior and the crucified Savior is often visualized in the traditional icons of the Nativity.

While those whom the shepherds told about the child were "amazed," Mary "treasured all these words and pondered them in her heart" (verses 18-19).

She engaged in deep reflection on what was taking place in a way that others did not. In contemplation she sought to put together her many thoughts into an understandable whole. This meditative pondering of the word of God is the invitation that Luke offers to all his readers.

Reflection and discussion

• What are some of the lessons Luke wants to teach his readers through the circumstances of Jesus' birth?

• Luke often describes God's salvation with a sense of joy. How does genuine joy permeate the narrative of the Savior's birth in the face of its obvious hardships?

• How does Mary teach me to treasure and ponder the word of God? What are the implications for reading Luke's gospel?

Prayer

God in the highest heaven, bring joy and peace to your people on earth. Help me to treasure and ponder your word so that I may understand your will and be an instrument of your salvation for others.

"For my eyes have seen your salvation, which you have prepared
in the presence of all peoples, a light for revelation to the Gentiles
and for glory to your people Israel." Luke 2:30-32

Salvation Prepared for Israel and the Gentiles

LUKE 2:22-40 ²²*When the time came for their purification according to the law of Moses, they brought him up to Jerusalem to present him to the Lord* ²³*(as it is written in the law of the Lord, "Every firstborn male shall be designated as holy to the Lord"),* ²⁴*and they offered a sacrifice according to what is stated in the law of the Lord, "a pair of turtledoves or two young pigeons."*

²⁵*Now there was a man in Jerusalem whose name was Simeon; this man was righteous and devout, looking forward to the consolation of Israel, and the Holy Spirit rested on him.* ²⁶*It had been revealed to him by the Holy Spirit that he would not see death before he had seen the Lord's Messiah.* ²⁷*Guided by the Spirit, Simeon came into the temple; and when the parents brought in the child Jesus, to do for him what was customary under the law,* ²⁸*Simeon took him in his arms and praised God, saying,*

²⁹*"Master, now you are dismissing your servant in peace,*
    according to your word;
³⁰*for my eyes have seen your salvation,*
    ³¹*which you have prepared in the presence of all peoples,*
³²*a light for revelation to the Gentiles*

and for glory to your people Israel."

[33] *And the child's father and mother were amazed at what was being said about him.* [34] *Then Simeon blessed them and said to his mother Mary, "This child is destined for the falling and the rising of many in Israel, and to be a sign that will be opposed* [35] *so that the inner thoughts of many will be revealed—and a sword will pierce your own soul too."*

[36] *There was also a prophet, Anna the daughter of Phanuel, of the tribe of Asher. She was of a great age, having lived with her husband seven years after her marriage,* [37] *then as a widow to the age of eighty-four. She never left the temple but worshiped there with fasting and prayer night and day.* [38] *At that moment she came, and began to praise God and to speak about the child to all who were looking for the redemption of Jerusalem.*

[39] *When they had finished everything required by the law of the Lord, they returned to Galilee, to their own town of Nazareth.* [40] *The child grew and became strong, filled with wisdom; and the favor of God was upon him.*

The infancy of Jesus, though part of a universal drama, takes place within the world of Judaism. Five times Luke observes that Mary and Joseph did everything required by the law of Israel (verses 22, 23, 24, 27, 39). He refers specifically to two separate regulations of the Torah: the purification of the mother forty days after the birth of a child (Lev 12:1-8) and the dedication of the firstborn son to God (Exod 13:2, 12-16). Mary and Joseph observed these rituals within the context of Jerusalem and its temple, the symbolic center of Israel's faith.

Simeon has been promised by the Holy Spirit that he would see the Messiah before his death (verse 26). Now, taking the six-week-old child Jesus in his arms, this devout, old man praises God for keeping his word. Simeon represents ancient Israel awaiting its Messiah with expectancy and hope. The old Israel can now rest in peace as the new age of God's salvation begins. As in the songs of Zechariah and Mary, the song of Simeon weaves his personal experience of God with what God is doing for all his people (verses 29-32). As God's salvation, Jesus is light both for the Gentiles and for Israel. This is the first explicit indication that the salvation offered in Jesus is directed to all people. Simeon's words are a preview of the saving drama that will continue throughout the gospel and Acts. Jesus is glory for the people of Israel and revelation to the Gentiles. He is the light of salvation to everyone on earth.

After this joyful song, Simeon speaks directly to Mary and prophesies that God's salvation will not be accomplished without great cost. He announces that Jesus is destined to be "a sign that will be opposed," an oracle that speaks of the division Jesus will cause and the rejection he will endure (verse 34). The "sign" given to the shepherds will lead to the sign of Jesus crucified and buried. He will be a sign that will provoke a divided response within Israel, a sign that some will accept and others will reject.

Then, almost as a whisper, he tells Mary that she will also pay a price for her intimate association with Jesus: "And a sword will pierce your own soul too" (verse 35). As both mother and disciple of Jesus, Mary will share in the pain and rejection Jesus will experience. She who was the first to hear and receive the good news will also experience within her own heart the full joy and grief of his saving life. As the ancient writers have said: "Great love means great pain."

Our Lady of Sorrows teaches us that grace is almost always accompanied by grief. A life pierced with affliction is a tragedy from one point of view, but the wounds of suffering can enlarge the human heart. As mother and disciple, Mary can teach us how to unite the sufferings of our lives with the cross of Christ, how to suffer in a way that enlarges our hearts and helps others see meaning and hope in the midst of pain.

Luke then turns his readers' attention to the testimony of a prophet named Anna. Remaining a widow after the early death of her husband, Anna chose a lifetime of service to God over remarriage. She is at the temple daily, fasting and offering prayers. Like Simeon, Anna points to Jesus and praises God for him. She addresses the crowd at the temple concerning the redemption of God's people. She testifies that God's decisive salvation has come in the child of Mary and Joseph. For those who await the consummation of God's saving plan, fulfillment has come.

Reflection and discussion

• What do Simeon and Anna have to teach me about the value found in waiting? How can I be patient and hopeful while I wait?

• How do the testimonies of Simeon and Anna indicate that the work of salvation includes both light and shadow? How is this demonstrated throughout the remainder of the gospel?

• How might Mary have felt when Simeon addressed the prophecy of the piercing sword to her? What does she teach me about suffering?

•What virtues do I see in Simeon and Anna? How could I put one of their qualities into practice in my own relationship with God?

Prayer

Lord and Master, you ask me to wait with patience and hope as your will is gradually unfolded. Give me a deep longing for your presence, and help me to trust that you are always faithful to the word of your promises.

Then Jesus went down with them and came to Nazareth, and was obedient to them. His mother treasured all these things in her heart. Luke 2:51

Jesus' Need to Be in His Father's House

LUKE 2:41-52 ⁴¹*Now every year his parents went to Jerusalem for the festival of the Passover.* ⁴²*And when he was twelve years old, they went up as usual for the festival.* ⁴³*When the festival was ended and they started to return, the boy Jesus stayed behind in Jerusalem, but his parents did not know it.* ⁴⁴*Assuming that he was in the group of travelers, they went a day's journey. Then they started to look for him among their relatives and friends.* ⁴⁵*When they did not find him, they returned to Jerusalem to search for him.* ⁴⁶*After three days they found him in the temple, sitting among the teachers, listening to them and asking them questions.* ⁴⁷*And all who heard him were amazed at his understanding and his answers.* ⁴⁸*When his parents saw him they were astonished; and his mother said to him, "Child, why have you treated us like this? Look, your father and I have been searching for you in great anxiety."* ⁴⁹*He said to them, "Why were you searching for me? Did you not know that I must be in my Father's house?"* ⁵⁰*But they did not understand what he said to them.* ⁵¹*Then he went down with them and came to Nazareth, and was obedient to them. His mother treasured all these things in her heart.*

⁵²*And Jesus increased in wisdom and in years, and in divine and human favor.*

This account of Jesus' adolescence is the only passage in the gospels that gives us a hint of Jesus' life from his birth to his baptism by John. The center of the narrative is Jesus' question, "Did you not know that I must be in my Father's house?" (verse 49). The passage may also be translated "involved in my Father's business" or "about my Father's work." For the first time in the gospel, Jesus calls God "my Father." However the passage is translated, the key idea is that as God's Son, the purpose and goal of Jesus' life is in relationship to his Father and in obedience to his will.

Mary's frantic search, reflected in her words "Son, why have you done this to us? Your father and I have been looking for you with great anxiety" (2:48), is the beginning of her life of sorrow in relationship to Jesus. Jesus seems pulled between the compliant obedience he owes his parents and a higher calling involving his unique relationship with God. Mary's heart was pierced with confusion, loss, and anxiety as she came to realize that all her hopes for her Son had to be readjusted in terms of the business of his Father. The loss of Jesus and his finding after three days (2:46) anticipates the death and resurrection of Jesus. For Mary, the loss of Jesus is only the beginning of a life in which she would continually submit her will to the ultimate destiny of Jesus with his Father.

In the temple of Jerusalem, the young Jesus seems to be teaching the teachers. Not only was Jesus asking them questions, but they were amazed at "his understanding and his answers" (verse 47). This prepares us for the climax of Jesus' adult ministry when, having reached the end of his journey to Jerusalem, he is found teaching in the temple by responding to the questions posed to him by the Jewish leaders (Luke 20–21).

These opening chapters of the gospel show us that Jesus is both Son of God and Son of Mary. Jesus returns to Nazareth with Joseph and Mary and is obedient to them (verse 51), yet he is also the obedient Son of his heavenly Father throughout his life. As Son of God and the Son of Mary, earth and heaven meet in him. Mary did not understand the things Jesus told her about directing his life to the Father (verse 50), but she accepted the mystery of the life and words of Jesus in the same way that she accepted the mystery of his conception and birth: she "treasured all these things in her heart" (verse 51). Through obedience to the ways of his earthly family—learning the Torah, observing the Sabbath, reflecting on the Scriptures, practicing the feasts of Israel—and through obedience to the mission given to him by the Father,

Jesus came to understand and embrace the purpose and goal of his life.

A true disciple is one who searches for the meaning of God's word, in spite of an inability to completely understand. By treasuring the word of God while pondering and meditating on it, the disciple is able to perceive increasingly deeper meanings and implications. A disciple is one who hears the word of God and then does the will of the Father.

Origen, a theologian of the third century, said: "Learn from Mary to seek Jesus." Mary's search for Jesus and finding him engaged in the work of his Father must also be our quest and our discovery. The disciple is one who seeks the Lord and who discovers that the way of Jesus is different from and beyond all our expectations. Seeking Jesus leads us to the house of the Father and to new and unexpected discoveries about the ways of God.

Reflection and discussion

• This account of Jesus, as he is between childhood and adulthood, reveals how Jesus understands his own life. How does Jesus see the motivation of his choices and the purpose of his mission?

• What about Jesus is most a mystery for me? What do I do when I am baffled by Jesus' words or deeds?

Prayer

Heavenly Father, help me to know that your business and your will must be the core of my life. Help me to imitate your Son so that I can be obedient both to the external commands of your word and to the inner urgings you instill within me.

SUGGESTIONS FOR GROUP SESSION 2

1. If there are newcomers who were not present for the first group session, introduce them now.

2. You may want to pray this prayer as a group:

Lord God, you chose Zechariah and Elizabeth, Joseph and Mary, Simeon and Anna, as instruments and heralds of the coming of your Son. May their patient waiting and hopeful expectation teach us to trust in your promises. As we study this gospel, may we treasure and ponder your word. Help us experience anew the grace of redemption which you brought to the world through Jesus, the Savior, Messiah, and Lord.

3. Ask one or more of the following questions:
   - What was your biggest challenge in Bible study over this past week?
   - What did you learn about yourself this week?

4. Discuss together lessons 1 through 6. Assuming that group members have read the Scripture and commentary during the week, there is no need to read it aloud. As you review each lesson, you might want to briefly summarize the Scripture passages of each lesson and ask the group what stands out most clearly from the commentary.

5. Choose one or more of the questions for reflection and discussion from each lesson to talk over as a group. You may want to ask group members which question was most challenging or helpful to them as you review each lesson.

6. Keep the discussion moving, but don't rush the discussion in order to complete more questions. Allow time for the questions that provoke the most discussion.

7. Instruct group members to complete lessons 7 through 12 on their own during the six days before the next group meeting. They should write out their own answers to the questions as preparation for next week's group discussion.

8. Conclude by praying aloud together the prayer at the end of lesson 6, or any other prayer you choose.

"Even now the ax is lying at the root of the trees; every tree therefore
that does not bear good fruit is cut down and thrown into the fire."
And the crowds asked him, "What then should we do?" Luke 3:9-10

Preaching and Promise
of John the Baptist

LUKE 3:1-20 ¹*In the fifteenth year of the reign of Emperor Tiberius, when
Pontius Pilate was governor of Judea, and Herod was ruler of Galilee, and his
brother Philip ruler of the region of Ituraea and Trachonitis, and Lysanias ruler
of Abilene, ²during the high priesthood of Annas and Caiaphas, the word of God
came to John son of Zechariah in the wilderness. ³He went into all the region
around the Jordan, proclaiming a baptism of repentance for the forgiveness of
sins, ⁴as it is written in the book of the words of the prophet Isaiah,*

"The voice of one crying out in the wilderness:
'Prepare the way of the Lord,
  make his paths straight.
⁵*Every valley shall be filled,*
  and every mountain and hill shall be made low,
and the crooked shall be made straight,
  and the rough ways made smooth;
⁶*and all flesh shall see the salvation of God.'"*

⁷*John said to the crowds that came out to be baptized by him, "You brood of
vipers! Who warned you to flee from the wrath to come? ⁸Bear fruits worthy of*

repentance. Do not begin to say to yourselves, 'We have Abraham as our ances-
tor'; for I tell you, God is able from these stones to raise up children to Abraham.
⁹Even now the ax is lying at the root of the trees; every tree therefore that does
not bear good fruit is cut down and thrown into the fire."

¹⁰And the crowds asked him, "What then should we do?" ¹¹In reply he said to
them, "Whoever has two coats must share with anyone who has none; and who-
ever has food must do likewise." ¹²Even tax collectors came to be baptized, and
they asked him, "Teacher, what should we do?" ¹³He said to them, "Collect no
more than the amount prescribed for you." ¹⁴Soldiers also asked him, "And we,
what should we do?" He said to them, "Do not extort money from anyone by
threats or false accusation, and be satisfied with your wages."

¹⁵As the people were filled with expectation, and all were questioning in their
hearts concerning John, whether he might be the Messiah, ¹⁶John answered all of
them by saying, "I baptize you with water; but one who is more powerful than
I is coming; I am not worthy to untie the thong of his sandals. He will baptize
you with the Holy Spirit and fire. ¹⁷His winnowing fork is in his hand, to clear
his threshing floor and to gather the wheat into his granary; but the chaff he will
burn with unquenchable fire."

¹⁸So, with many other exhortations, he proclaimed the good news to the peo-
ple. ¹⁹But Herod the ruler, who had been rebuked by him because of Herodias,
his brother's wife, and because of all the evil things that Herod had done, ²⁰added
to them all by shutting up John in prison.

Luke introduces John the Baptist by listing the imperial and local rulers who governed during his ministry, reminiscent of the style of ancient historians and the preface of Old Testament prophets (Isa 1:1; Jer 1:1-3). The detailed list highlights the universal perspective of Luke's gospel. As attested by the long line of Israel's prophets, "the word of God" came to John (verse 2).

John begins his ministry in the wilderness, traveling "into all the region around the Jordan" River (verse 3). He comes, as the ancient Scriptures promised, to announce the way of the Lord and to baptize for the forgiveness of sins. His message prepares the people for the coming of salvation with a call to repent. This repentance is a reorientation of one's perspective, from sin to the sovereignty of God. It is an internal attitude that produces external actions that manifest a sense of responsibility before God.

Luke expresses the significance of John's ministry by describing it as a fulfillment of Isaiah 40:3-5. As a prologue for the whole of Isaiah's message (Isa 40–66), the clearing of the way prepares for God's coming with his final salvation. The straight paths are the purified hearts of God's people. The preparation portrays a new exodus, the fundamental pattern of God's salvation. Just as God led his people in the wilderness, parting the sea before them, God removes all obstacles for them as he delivers them from bondage. Of all the gospels, only Luke concludes the citation of Isaiah with a universal focus: "and all flesh shall see the salvation of God" (verse 6). This focus on all people, not just the people of Israel, is a crucial emphasis of Luke. God's salvation, which is found in Jesus, is available to all.

As a fiery preacher of morality, John the Baptist called people to produce deeds appropriate to their repentance; words without concrete action mean nothing (verse 8). With the coming of salvation's hope, the time of judgment also draws near. Repentance is necessary in order to escape God's wrath. The axe is ready to fall on the fruitless trees, a graphic warning for those who fail to discern the urgency of the times. "The children of Abraham," those who respond and choose God, are not limited to a certain racial or religious heritage. Inner transformation from the heart creates God's children. Submitting to John's baptism expresses this inner reorientation while waiting for God salvation.

"What then should we do?" ask the three groups of people who come to John: the crowds, the tax collectors, and the soldiers. Sharing what you have with the needy; conducting yourselves honorably; giving up gouging, blackmail, and extortion; not leaving others destitute for your own gains; and being content with what you have (verses 10-14)—these are the good fruit people must produce if they are not to be like barren trees that are cut off at the roots (verse 9) or like the chaff thrown into the fire (verse 17). This sample of John's call to repentance invites everyone to consider how they are called to repent and prepare for the coming of the Lord.

The prophetic ministry of John is only the prelude for the public ministry of Jesus. John's work stirs up hope of deliverance in his Jewish audience sensitive to the message of their ancient Scripture. The "one who is more powerful" than John is the real promise and hope. In contrast to John's baptism with water stands Jesus' baptism with the Holy Spirit and fire. The winnowing fork lifts the produce in the air at harvest time. As the divine wind blows across the threshing floor, the good grain falls to the ground and is saved for the granary while the useless chaff is gathered and burned up.

John exhorted the people in many other ways, but finally, like so many prophets before him, he is arrested and imprisoned. Herod regarded John as a threat because John had criticized his lifestyle and his marriage to Herodias. Herod represents the tragedy of those who reject John's call to repentance. Unable to tolerate having his sin exposed, even when forgiveness is offered, Herod seeks to destroy God's messenger. John has prepared the way; God's salvation is now at hand. Now the time of fulfillment can begin with the ministry of Jesus.

Reflection and discussion

• Why is the wilderness the ideal place for God's people to prepare themselves for the coming of salvation?

• In what ways do Isaiah and John the Baptist describe the coming of God as a new exodus for God's people?

Prayer

Lord God, you call me to repent of my sin in order to prepare the way for you. Clear away all the obstacles that prevent me from experiencing your saving power so that I can receive your salvation.

When Jesus also had been baptized and was praying, the heaven was opened, and the Holy Spirit descended upon him in bodily form like a dove.
Luke 3:21-22

Son of Adam, Son of God

LUKE 3:21-38 *²¹Now when all the people were baptized, and when Jesus also had been baptized and was praying, the heaven was opened, ²²and the Holy Spirit descended upon him in bodily form like a dove. And a voice came from heaven, "You are my Son, the Beloved; with you I am well pleased."*

²³Jesus was about thirty years old when he began his work. He was the son (as was thought) of Joseph son of Heli, ²⁴son of Matthat, son of Levi, son of Melchi, son of Jannai, son of Joseph, ²⁵son of Mattathias, son of Amos, son of Nahum, son of Esli, son of Naggai, ²⁶son of Maath, son of Mattathias, son of Semein, son of Josech, son of Joda, ²⁷son of Joanan, son of Rhesa, son of Zerubbabel, son of Shealtiel, son of Neri, ²⁸son of Melchi, son of Addi, son of Cosam, son of Elmadam, son of Er, ²⁹son of Joshua, son of Eliezer, son of Jorim, son of Matthat, son of Levi, ³⁰son of Simeon, son of Judah, son of Joseph, son of Jonam, son of Eliakim, ³¹son of Melea, son of Menna, son of Mattatha, son of Nathan, son of David, ³²son of Jesse, son of Obed, son of Boaz, son of Sala, son of Nahshon, ³³son of Amminadab, son of Admin, son of Arni, son of Hezron, son of Perez, son of Judah, ³⁴son of Jacob, son of Isaac, son of Abraham, son of Terah, son of Nahor, ³⁵son of Serug, son of Reu, son of Peleg, son of Eber, son of Shelah, ³⁶son of Cainan, son of Arphaxad, son of Shem, son of Noah, son of Lamech, ³⁷son of Methuselah, son of Enoch, son of Jared, son of Mahalaleel, son of Cainan, ³⁸son of Enos, son of Seth, son of Adam, son of God.

Jesus' choice to receive the baptism of John expresses his support of John's message and ministry, and it expresses his solidarity with sinful and repentant humanity. Yet, in comparison to the other gospels, Luke underplays the baptism. He does not describe the baptism, but focuses on what happens afterward, while Jesus is praying. The opening of heaven expresses a dramatic revelation of God in the world of humanity. Here God's revelation is expressed in the sign of the Holy Spirit descending on Jesus and the heavenly testimony about Jesus.

The descending Spirit "in bodily form" is not a dove, but comes like the graceful movement of a dove (verse 22). At the annunciation, the divine Spirit comes upon Mary and overshadows her, and at Pentecost, the Spirit will come like a rushing wind, and tongues as of fire will rest upon the people. The symbolism gives narrative expression to the transforming presence of the Holy Spirit. The voice of God confirms that Jesus is his beloved Son in whom he delights. He is the one to whom John the Baptist looked. His mission is rooted in his identity as Son of God, and he will carry it out anointed by the Holy Spirit.

Luke notes that Jesus was about thirty years old when he began his public ministry (verse 23). Turning thirty held great significance for many in ancient Israel. This is the age at which priests began serving in the temple (Num 4:3; 1 Chron 23:3) and the age at which Ezekiel began his work as a prophet (Ezek 1:1). Most significantly, thirty was the age at which David began his reign (2 Samuel 5:4. Since Jesus, as Israel's Messiah, is shown to be a priest, prophet, and king, the age of thirty seems appropriate for the inauguration of his saving mission.

Unlike Matthew's gospel, which begins with the genealogy of Jesus, Luke places the genealogy after the baptism of Jesus and before his temptation in the wilderness. The reality that ties together all three of these passages is the identity of Jesus as the Son of God. At his baptism, the voice from heaven revealed him to be God's Son. The climax of the genealogy is the final phrase, "son of Adam, son of God" (verse 38). And in the temptation account, the devil demands that Jesus prove he is the Son of God.

As Luke begins listing the ancestry of Jesus, beginning with Joseph, he notes in parentheses, "as was thought" (verse 23). Joseph was commonly assumed to be the natural father of Jesus by those who did not know that Jesus was conceived through the Holy Spirit. Luke's notation clarifies that this is the legal genealogy of Jesus since, from the point of view of the law of Israel, Jesus was Joseph's son and heir and, like him, a descendant of David. Most of the other names in the list of ancestors are unknown until the mention of David. Then from David to Jacob, Isaac, and Abraham, the list has many similarities to Matthew's genealogy.

Finally, the most notable difference is that Luke extends the ancestry past Abraham, all the way back to Adam. According to Genesis, the whole human race descends from Adam. By extending the genealogy to Adam, Luke highlights the identification of Jesus with all humanity, stressing the fact that Jesus is significant not only for the "children of Abraham" (3:8), but for all the descendants of Adam. This universal emphasis fits the concern of Luke that Jesus is the Savior of all people, both Jews and Gentiles.

Reflection and discussion

• Why does Luke take note of the age of Jesus as he began his ministry? What is significant about age thirty in my own life?

• What does Jesus' ancestry tell me about him? In what way does my ancestry tell who I am? In what ways does my ancestry fail to identify my uniqueness?

Prayer

Father of Jesus, you have called me to follow your plan and have anointed me with power by your Holy Spirit. Help me to live as your child and to express the commitment of my baptism with words and deeds.

**When the devil had finished every test,
he departed from him until an opportune time.** Luke 4:13

Resistance to Temptation

LUKE 4:1-13 ¹*Jesus, full of the Holy Spirit, returned from the Jordan and was led by the Spirit in the wilderness,* ²*where for forty days he was tempted by the devil. He ate nothing at all during those days, and when they were over, he was famished.* ³*The devil said to him, "If you are the Son of God, command this stone to become a loaf of bread."* ⁴*Jesus answered him, "It is written, 'One does not live by bread alone.'"*

⁵*Then the devil led him up and showed him in an instant all the kingdoms of the world.* ⁶*And the devil said to him, "To you I will give their glory and all this authority; for it has been given over to me, and I give it to anyone I please.* ⁷*If you, then, will worship me, it will all be yours."* ⁸*Jesus answered him, "It is written,*

*'Worship the Lord your God,
    and serve only him.'"*

⁹*Then the devil took him to Jerusalem, and placed him on the pinnacle of the temple, saying to him, "If you are the Son of God, throw yourself down from here,* ¹⁰*for it is written,*

*'He will command his angels concerning you,
    to protect you,'*

¹¹*and*

'On their hands they will bear you up,

45

so that you will not dash your foot against a stone.'"
¹²*Jesus answered him, "It is said, 'Do not put the Lord your God to the test.'"*
¹³*When the devil had finished every test, he departed from him until an opportune time.*

The fact that Jesus experiences temptation immediately after the glorious revelation at his baptism convinces us that he was not exempt from a life of trials and temptations. Jesus, like all of us, experienced the pains of real hunger, and, when he was physically weak, he experienced real temptations. Although he is the Son of God, he is also the son of Adam, a member of humanity.

Perhaps another reason that Luke inserted his genealogy immediately before the temptations of Jesus is to contrast the success of Jesus in overcoming demonic temptations with the failure of Adam. Where humanity was tempted and overcome by sin, Jesus, the new Adam, shows unswerving obedience to God. The account demonstrates that Jesus overcame the three great vices: love of pleasure, love of possessions, and love of glory. His refusal to be mastered by any of these vices convinces us that he is a great moral teacher, an example for us of discipline and dedication to God's will. As the letter to the Hebrews says of him, "Because he himself was tested by what he suffered, he is able to help those who are being tested" (Heb 2:18).

Filled with the Holy Spirit and led by the Spirit to the place of testing, Jesus overcomes the evil he faces by his reflective application of the truths of Scripture. When he is tempted to provide food for himself from a stone, Jesus counters with a quote from Deuteronomy, reminding Israel to trust in God's faithfulness and protection (Deut 8:3). When the devil offers to give Jesus all the wealth and power of the world's kingdoms in exchange for Jesus' allegiance to him, Jesus replies with another passage from Deuteronomy, commanding God's people to worship and serve only God (Deut 6:13). Finally, when Jesus is tempted to demonstrate his power by casting himself down from the temple, making a flashy display of his power and glory, Jesus responds with another command from Deuteronomy, "Do not put the Lord your God to the test" (Deut 6:16).

The forty days of fasting in the wilderness recalls the forty-day fast of Moses before writing the words of the covenant (Exod 34:28) and the forty-day journey of Elijah through the wilderness (1 Kings 19:8). The temptations also recall the Israelites' forty years of wandering in this same wilderness. The book of Deuteronomy describes that period as a time in which God tested his people: "The Lord your God has led you these forty years in the wilderness, in order to humble you, testing you to know what was in your heart, whether or not you would keep his commandments" (Deut 8:2). The temptations recall Israel's failures as they are contrasted with the success of Jesus in overcoming the satanic tests. Alone in the wilderness, where no human could observe and where only God could see him, Jesus showed himself to be the obedient Son of God.

These tests of Jesus are repeated continually in the lives of all his followers, just as they express the kinds of temptations that Israel encountered in the exodus. Jesus shows that he is ready for the ministry that the Father has given to him, and Luke shows his readers the way to live faithfully with God. This fidelity involves trusting God, worshiping him alone, and refusing to test his goodness. Disciples of Jesus must walk in God's ways and trust in God's will, even when it entails suffering and self-denial.

At the end of the testing, Luke tells us that the devil departs from Jesus, but adds the provocative phrase, "until an opportune time." Luke's account of Jesus' ministry is filled with demonic challenges, as Jesus vanquishes Satan and evil spirits throughout the gospel. These challenges will intensify as Jesus approaches his passion, and Satan will attack again when Jesus is again weakened by disappointment and suffering.

Reflection and discussion

• Why did Luke place this temptation account immediately after ending Jesus' genealogy with Adam? In what sense do these tests represent the enticements of all people?

• How did Jesus use his prayerful reflection on Scripture in these times of testing? How can Scripture help me when I am tempted to compromise my allegiance to God or demand that God act according to my own scripts?

• If the devil was going to tempt me most effectively, what three temptations would he use? How do these compare to the temptations of Jesus?

• In what ways am I tempted to use God's gifts for myself rather than for God's purposes?

Prayer

Lord God, you lead me with your Holy Spirit through suffering, struggle, and temptation. Give me strength to fight temptation, and give me a deep desire to know and do your will. Help me to be faithful to you even when I am weakest.

When they heard this, all in the synagogue were filled with rage. They got up, drove him out of the town, and led him to the brow of the hill on which their town was built, so that they might hurl him off the cliff. Luke 4:28-29

The Rejection of Jesus at Nazareth

LUKE 4:14-30 ¹⁴*Then Jesus, filled with the power of the Spirit, returned to Galilee, and a report about him spread through all the surrounding country.* ¹⁵*He began to teach in their synagogues and was praised by everyone.*

¹⁶*When he came to Nazareth, where he had been brought up, he went to the synagogue on the sabbath day, as was his custom. He stood up to read,* ¹⁷*and the scroll of the prophet Isaiah was given to him. He unrolled the scroll and found the place where it was written:*

¹⁸*"The Spirit of the Lord is upon me,*
because he has anointed me to bring good news to the poor.
He has sent me to proclaim release to the captives
and recovery of sight to the blind,
to let the oppressed go free,
¹⁹*to proclaim the year of the Lord's favor."*

²⁰*And he rolled up the scroll, gave it back to the attendant, and sat down. The eyes of all in the synagogue were fixed on him.* ²¹*Then he began to say to them, "Today this scripture has been fulfilled in your hearing."* ²²*All spoke well of him and were amazed at the gracious words that came from his mouth. They said,*

"Is not this Joseph's son?" [23]*He said to them, "Doubtless you will quote to me this proverb, 'Doctor, cure yourself!' And you will say, 'Do here also in your hometown the things that we have heard you did at Capernaum.'"* [24]*And he said, "Truly I tell you, no prophet is accepted in the prophet's hometown.* [25]*But the truth is, there were many widows in Israel in the time of Elijah, when the heaven was shut up three years and six months, and there was a severe famine over all the land;* [26]*yet Elijah was sent to none of them except to a widow at Zarephath in Sidon.* [27]*There were also many lepers in Israel in the time of the prophet Elisha, and none of them was cleansed except Naaman the Syrian."* [28]*When they heard this, all in the synagogue were filled with rage.* [29]*They got up, drove him out of the town, and led him to the brow of the hill on which their town was built, so that they might hurl him off the cliff.* [30]*But he passed through the midst of them and went on his way.*

Still under the empowerment and guidance of the Holy Spirit, Jesus returns to Galilee where he begins his public ministry by teaching in the synagogues of the area. The synagogues, as places where the Jewish people assembled for prayer, Scripture reading, instruction, and discussion, were the natural settings for Jesus to present his teachings. Since instruction was primarily the interpretation of Scripture and Jesus was well versed in the Torah and prophets of Israel, he instructed the assembly at these Sabbath gatherings. His fame spread throughout the region and he was praised by those who heard him.

As Jesus comes to his hometown of Nazareth, we see an example of the kind of teaching Jesus is offering throughout the synagogues of the region. He sees his own ministry as a natural completion of Judaism's hope, so he desires all Jews to enter this time of fulfillment. In the passage that he reads from the scroll of the prophet Isaiah, the anointed Servant of God announces release to all those in bondage (Isa 61:1-2). The liberation echoes, but is far greater than, the exodus from Egypt and the return from Babylon. The deliverance that the prophetic Servant proclaims is marked by four infinitives: to bring good news to the poor, to proclaim liberty to captives and sight to the blind, to let the oppressed go free, and to proclaim the year of the Lord's favor.

Jews at the time of Jesus would have understood this passage to refer to the coming of God's new age of salvation, so its proclamation by Jesus catches the attention of his listeners as they wait to hear his instruction. As Jesus sat down, the customary position for teaching, he begins with the words, "Today this scripture has been fulfilled in your hearing" (verse 21). He is stating that the total deliverance that Isaiah describes is now put into motion with his coming. Jesus himself is the truest Servant of God. He is the one anointed with God's Spirit to be the bearer of God's salvation to his people.

Those who are poor, captive, blind, or oppressed understand their own needs and respond more directly and honestly to God's message of hope than those who are not so subjugated. The imagery of deliverance echoes the description of the Jubilee year (Lev 25:8-17), when debts were canceled and slaves were liberated. Jesus' announcement of "the year of the Lord's favor" indicates the arrival of the time when the spiritual debt of sin will be forgiven and when those held in the bondage of sickness and evil will be freed. The words and deeds of Jesus throughout the rest of Luke's gospel indicate that this proclamation of Isaiah is a prologue to his saving ministry.

The mood of the crowd shifts dramatically in this passage. After Jesus proclaimed the Scripture passage fulfilled, "all spoke well of him and were amazed" (verse 22). But when the people of Nazareth demand that Jesus do the things in his hometown that he has done elsewhere, they become skeptical and then furious. Jesus recalls how the prophets of Israel were rejected by their own people. He offers examples from the lives of Elijah and Elisha, showing how the rejection of the prophets in Israel led them to go beyond the borders of their own people and interact with the Gentiles. Jesus is prophesying how those closest to him will miss God's salvation, while others who are far away will receive it. By this point, "all in the synagogue were filled with rage" and wanted to hurl him off a cliff. God's blessing for the Gentiles was too much for his audience to bear, so they rejected his message and his ministry.

Reflection and discussion

• The synagogue service on the Sabbath consisted of prayers, a reading from the Torah, a reading from the prophets, instructions on the Scriptures, and a blessing. What are some similarities to Christian liturgy today?

• How does Jesus' instruction on Isaiah 61 indicate that healing, forgiveness, and liberation are all aspects of God's salvation?

• In what ways am I poor, captive, blind, and oppressed? Do I believe that Jesus wants to grant me release and forgiveness from all that holds me captive?

• Why does the mood of all in the synagogue change so radically? In what ways might God's generosity enrage people today?

Prayer

Lord God, your Son announced good news to the poor, captive, blind, and oppressed. I thank you for the salvation you offer to every person. Don't let me ever be jealous of your generosity to others, and help me accept with gratitude the grace you give to me.

"I must proclaim the good news of the kingdom of God to the other cities also; for I was sent for this purpose." Luke 4:43

Examples of Jesus' Ministry

LUKE 4:31-44 *31He went down to Capernaum, a city in Galilee, and was teaching them on the sabbath. 32They were astounded at his teaching, because he spoke with authority. 33In the synagogue there was a man who had the spirit of an unclean demon, and he cried out with a loud voice, 34"Let us alone! What have you to do with us, Jesus of Nazareth? Have you come to destroy us? I know who you are, the Holy One of God." 35But Jesus rebuked him, saying, "Be silent, and come out of him!" When the demon had thrown him down before them, he came out of him without having done him any harm. 36They were all amazed and kept saying to one another, "What kind of utterance is this? For with authority and power he commands the unclean spirits, and out they come!" 37And a report about him began to reach every place in the region.*

38After leaving the synagogue he entered Simon's house. Now Simon's mother-in-law was suffering from a high fever, and they asked him about her. 39Then he stood over her and rebuked the fever, and it left her. Immediately she got up and began to serve them.

40As the sun was setting, all those who had any who were sick with various kinds of diseases brought them to him; and he laid his hands on each of them and cured them. 41Demons also came out of many, shouting, "You are the Son of God!" But he rebuked them and would not allow them to speak, because they knew that he was the Messiah.

⁴²At daybreak he departed and went into a deserted place. And the crowds were looking for him; and when they reached him, they wanted to prevent him from leaving them. ⁴³But he said to them, "I must proclaim the good news of the kingdom of God to the other cities also; for I was sent for this purpose." ⁴⁴So he continued proclaiming the message in the synagogues of Judea.

T
he prophetic call of Isaiah to bring "release to the captives" and "to let the oppressed go free" begins to be carried out in the words and deeds of Jesus. Luke provides us with a glimpse of a typical Sabbath in Jesus' ministry in Capernaum. In a rapid series of scenes, we see Jesus teaching with authority (verses 31-32), casting out an unclean demon (verses 33-35), curing Peter's mother-in-law (verses 38-39), and healing many other sick and possessed people (verses 40-41).

The scenes show a close connection between Jesus' teachings and his healings. In his instructions, exorcisms, and cures, the people are amazed at the "authority" with which he speaks (verses 32, 36). He is not just another charismatic teacher, positive thinker, or great motivator. He is the one with the authority to defeat the evil forces that can dominate humanity.

Luke also shows us the close connection between the authority to cast out evil spirits and the power to cure afflictions. Just as Jesus "rebuked" the demons (verses 35, 41) and they departed, Jesus "rebuked" the fever of Peter's mother-in-law, and it departed (verse 39). In both scenes Jesus cast out whatever was keeping the person captive and preventing the person from experiencing genuine freedom.

In each example of Jesus' work, Luke points out the particular concern Jesus has for each individual as he heals them one by one. His compassion makes him approachable and gives people confidence to ask him for help in their need. Even when Jesus is surrounded by a crowd of people in need, Luke notes that he "laid his hands on each of them and cured them" (verse 40). Luke invites his readers into the scenes to witness these events, and we are asked to imagine what it would be like to listen to Jesus, to receive his healing touch, to be freed from bondage to evil, and then to feel amazed and grateful for God's salvation.

All of Jesus' activities, his teaching and healing, are ways of proclaiming "the good news of the kingdom of God" (verse 43). This proclamation of

God's kingdom is a summary of the mission of Jesus; it is the "purpose" for which Jesus is sent. Throughout the gospel, Luke shows that this kingdom contains both present and future elements. Some passages demonstrate its nearness or its having come in Jesus, while others look to the total manifestation of God's rule in the final age. Nevertheless, Jesus must continue to proclaim the good news, in word and in deed, throughout Galilee and Judea.

The challenge of making known the good news of God's kingdom is a task that Jesus wishes to share with his disciples. Now that his mission is made clear, Luke will show us how Jesus calls his disciples to follow him and gives them the same authority to preach the kingdom, to cast out demons, and to cure the sick (9:1-2). As disciples, we too are empowered by Jesus to proclaim release to captives, to lead the oppressed to freedom, to witness and heal, and to proclaim the good news in word and deed.

Reflection and discussion

• What is the link between the teachings and healings of Jesus? How does Luke show this deep connection?

• How does the gospel demonstrate Jesus' care and compassion for each individual? How can disciples of Jesus show this particular concern for each person?

Prayer

Lord God, you release captives through the authority and power you gave Jesus to heal. I ask you to heal me from my afflictions so that I can proclaim the good news of your kingdom in the world. Help me to be an instrument of your healing for others.

Jesus said to Simon, "Do not be afraid; from now on you will be catching people." When they had brought their boats to shore, they left everything and followed him. Luke 5:10-11

An Abundant Catch at the Word of Jesus

LUKE 5:1-11 ¹*Once while Jesus was standing beside the lake of Gennesaret, and the crowd was pressing in on him to hear the word of God, ²he saw two boats there at the shore of the lake; the fishermen had gone out of them and were washing their nets. ³He got into one of the boats, the one belonging to Simon, and asked him to put out a little way from the shore. Then he sat down and taught the crowds from the boat. ⁴When he had finished speaking, he said to Simon, "Put out into the deep water and let down your nets for a catch." ⁵Simon answered, "Master, we have worked all night long but have caught nothing. Yet if you say so, I will let down the nets." ⁶When they had done this, they caught so many fish that their nets were beginning to break. ⁷So they signaled their partners in the other boat to come and help them. And they came and filled both boats, so that they began to sink. ⁸But when Simon Peter saw it, he fell down at Jesus' knees, saying, "Go away from me, Lord, for I am a sinful man!" ⁹For he and all who were with him were amazed at the catch of fish that they had taken; ¹⁰and so also were James and John, sons of Zebedee, who were partners with Simon. Then Jesus said to Simon, "Do not be afraid; from now on you will be* *catching people."* [11] *When they had brought their boats to shore, they left everything and followed him.*

The fishermen are washing their nets after fishing all night. Jesus gets into the boat of Simon Peter and asks him to row out into the lake so that Jesus can preach to the crowd. Since voices travel well across the water, Jesus is able to escape from the pressing crowds on the shore and still teach them from the boat.

Luke refers to the teaching of Jesus as "the word of God" (5:1). The expression emphasizes not only the divine source of Jesus' words but also the authority of his message. God's word, manifested by Jesus in his preaching and teaching, is also displayed in action.

Jesus instructs Peter to row out to the deep water and lower the nets for a catch. Peter's objection to Jesus' words—"Master, we have worked all night long and have caught nothing"—and then his acceptance—"Yet if you say so, I will let down the nets"—echoes Mary's objection (1:34) and her acceptance of the word of God (1:38). Mary's acceptance—"let it be with me according to your word"—marks the beginning of the new age of salvation; Peter's acceptance marks the beginning of Christian discipleship. At all the critical moments of Luke's gospel, we see that God's ways always surprise us and reverse our human expectations. Peter's astonishment at the catch of fish they had made (verse 9) expresses again the wondrous reality that Mary observed, that "nothing will be impossible with God" (1:37).

Luke focuses his attention on Peter throughout the gospel and into the Acts of the Apostles. He is the first disciple chosen by Jesus and is the most important disciple within Jesus' inner circle. Jesus' first command, to "put out a little way from the shore," is singular and is addressed to Peter, who is steering the vessel. But the second command, to "let down your nets for a catch," is plural and invites Peter's companions to help in casting the nets and bringing in the catch. Although Peter is in charge of the boat, he calls Jesus Master and demonstrates an understanding of his authority. Trusting in his Master, Peter gives the command to cast the nets.

Casting the nets meets with great success, yet the nets were so full that they were beginning to break. When James and John brought their boat to help with the catch, both boats were filled until they began to sink. Divine knowledge and authority is present through Jesus. The word of God, spoken by Jesus, is powerful and effective. Jesus knows the vocation and needs of the fishermen better than they themselves. Even in the strain and turmoil that results, trusting in and depending on Jesus provides for abundance.

Peter's feeling of unworthiness at receiving God's bounty and in the presence of God's authority leads him to fall down at the knees of Jesus (verse 8). Peter's humble perception of himself as a sinner before the Lord shows his insightful understanding of the greatness of Jesus and humanity's condition. At first Peter thinks that his sin means that he can have nothing to do with Jesus. But Jesus shows how the realization that one is a sinner is fundamental to discipleship and spiritual growth. He takes the faith and humble attitude of Peter and transforms them into a call to serve.

Jesus' words to Peter—"from now on you will be catching people" (verse 10)—assure Peter and his partners of their new vocation as apostles. They will rescue people from evil and gather them into the nets of God's kingdom. Their mission is evangelization—offering the gospel to people and inviting them into a new, vibrant, and purposeful life. At the height of the greatest catch of their lives, they leave their profession behind to follow Jesus and to fish for people.

Reflection and discussion

• Jesus uses Peter's boat as a pulpit from which to cast the net of the gospel over his hearers. In what way are the boat and the net outstanding images of the church and its ministry?

• What qualities of Peter does Jesus use to make him a disciple?

• How has God called me to accept his plan despite my objections? What does Jesus ask me to leave behind in order to follow him?

• Jesus said to Peter, "Do not be afraid; from now on you will be catching people." What is the meaning of this statement for the life of Peter?

Prayer

Holy God, you work marvels that astonish your people and draw them to you. Your Son has called me to follow him and to evangelize your people. Lead me to accept his invitation to proclaim your kingdom in word and in action.

SUGGESTIONS FOR FACILITATORS, GROUP SESSION 3

1. Welcome group members and ask if there are any announcements anyone would like to make.

2. You may want to pray this prayer as a group:

Father of our Lord Jesus Christ, through baptism you have anointed us with the Holy Spirit and given us a share in your life. Through suffering, struggle, and temptation, you lead us to a deeper understanding of your will for us. Help us to realize our own poverty, blindness, weakness, and sin, so that we will be always ready to accept with gratitude your invitation to salvation. Heal me from all the obstacles that prevent me from experiencing the fullness of your life so that I can proclaim the good news of your kingdom in the world.

3. Ask one or more of the following questions:
   • Which image from lessons 7–12 stands out most memorably to you?
   • What is the most important thing you learned through your study this week?

4. Discuss lessons 7 through 12. Choose one or more of the questions for reflection and discussion from each lesson to discuss as a group. You may want to ask group members which question was most challenging or helpful to them as you review each lesson.

5. Remember that there are no definitive answers for these discussion questions. The insights of group members will add to the understanding of all. None of these questions require an expert.

6. After talking about each lesson, instruct group members to complete lessons 13 through 18 on their own during the six days before the next group meeting. They should write out their own answers to the questions as preparation for next week's group discussion.

7. Ask the group if anyone is having any particular problems with the Bible study during the week. You may want to share advice and encouragement within the group.

8. Conclude by praying aloud together the prayer at the end of one of the lessons discussed. You may add to the prayer based on the sharing that has occurred in the group.

"Those who are well have no need of a physician, but those who are sick; I have come to call not the righteous but sinners to repentance." Luke 5:31-32

Healing to the Sick and Forgiveness to Sinners

LUKE 5:12-32 [12]*Once, when he was in one of the cities, there was a man covered with leprosy. When he saw Jesus, he bowed with his face to the ground and begged him, "Lord, if you choose, you can make me clean."* [13]*Then Jesus stretched out his hand, touched him, and said, "I do choose. Be made clean." Immediately the leprosy left him.* [14]*And he ordered him to tell no one. "Go," he said, "and show yourself to the priest, and, as Moses commanded, make an offering for your cleansing, for a testimony to them."* [15]*But now more than ever the word about Jesus spread abroad; many crowds would gather to hear him and to be cured of their diseases.* [16]*But he would withdraw to deserted places and pray.*

[17]*One day, while he was teaching, Pharisees and teachers of the law were sitting near by (they had come from every village of Galilee and Judea and from Jerusalem); and the power of the Lord was with him to heal.* [18]*Just then some men came, carrying a paralyzed man on a bed. They were trying to bring him in and lay him before Jesus;* [19]*but finding no way to bring him in because of the crowd, they went up on the roof and let him down with his bed through the tiles into the middle of the crowd in front of Jesus.* [20]*When he saw their faith, he said, "Friend, your sins are forgiven you."* [21]*Then the scribes and the Pharisees began to question, "Who is this who is speaking blasphemies? Who can forgive sins but*

God alone?" ²²When Jesus perceived their questionings, he answered them, "Why do you raise such questions in your hearts? ²³Which is easier, to say, 'Your sins are forgiven you,' or to say, 'Stand up and walk'? ²⁴But so that you may know that the Son of Man has authority on earth to forgive sins" —he said to the one who was paralyzed—"I say to you, stand up and take your bed and go to your home." ²⁵Immediately he stood up before them, took what he had been lying on, and went to his home, glorifying God. ²⁶Amazement seized all of them, and they glorified God and were filled with awe, saying, "We have seen strange things today."

²⁷After this he went out and saw a tax collector named Levi, sitting at the tax booth; and he said to him, "Follow me." ²⁸And he got up, left everything, and followed him.

²⁹Then Levi gave a great banquet for him in his house; and there was a large crowd of tax collectors and others sitting at the table with them. ³⁰The Pharisees and their scribes were complaining to his disciples, saying, "Why do you eat and drink with tax collectors and sinners?" ³¹Jesus answered, "Those who are well have no need of a physician, but those who are sick; ³²I have come to call not the righteous but sinners to repentance."

These healing narratives continue to demonstrate the powerful authority of Jesus and his compassionate care for those in need. The man "covered with leprosy" is a person cast out from society because of his contagion. As specified by Leviticus 13–14, a leper is considered unclean and is removed from the ordinary life of the people as long as the disease lasts. Despite these prohibitions, the leper bows before Jesus, addressing him as Lord. He knows that God is working through Jesus, and the leper implores him, "Lord, if you choose, you can make me clean" (verse 12). The request centers not on Jesus' ability, but on his willingness to heal.

Jesus responds with a gentle touch and assuring words. The leper both hears and feels Jesus' willingness to make him whole. Jesus' word would have been sufficient, but his touch expresses his compassion and confirms his care. The words and touch of Jesus immediately cause the disease to leave the man, but Jesus downplays his miraculous work. He commands the healed man to present himself to the priests at the temple and to offer sacrifice for his cleansing as the Torah requires (verse 14). The reason for this command is so that the man may be a "testimony" for the religious leadership in Jerusalem that God is at work in Jesus.

The result of this healing is the gathering of larger crowds around Jesus. The news about Jesus has continued to spread, first around the towns of Galilee, and now it has even reached the highest levels in Judea and Jerusalem (verse 17). Among the crowds who come to seek out Jesus are some Pharisees and teachers of the law. For the first time, Jesus prepares to confront some of the officials of organized Judaism.

Getting access to Jesus proved to be increasingly difficult, so the ingenious friends of a paralyzed man make a hole in the clay roof and let him down in front of Jesus (verse 19). Their persistent effort leads Jesus to again demonstrate his healing authority. This time, rather than healing the man's external illness, Jesus says, "Your sins are forgiven you." With this, Jesus begins to demonstrate that his mission carries a message about deeper, spiritual realities. Disease and sin both demonstrate the disorder within creation and evil in the world. Forgiving sins is a greater healing than a physical cure; in fact, sin is the worst of all diseases. Jesus' claim to forgive sins shows the comprehensiveness of his saving mission.

The scribes and Pharisees begin raising questions about Jesus within their hearts, the beginning of a process that will lead to Jesus' conviction (verses 21-22). Their charge that Jesus is speaking blasphemies suggests that he is claiming a divine prerogative and thereby violating God's majesty. So in order to substantiate his claim to forgive sins, Jesus orders the paralytic to stand up, take his bed, and go home. The effectiveness of Jesus' healing words to cure the paralytic in an observable way demonstrates the power of his word to heal people's inner heart and spirit. The paralytic immediately obeys, the observers are filled with awe, and they all glorify God with gratitude and joy for his saving work among them.

Jesus' outreach to outcasts continues with his call to Levi at his tax booth. Tax collectors were held in low esteem and generally rejected in the Jewish culture for collaborating with their oppressors. Levi leaves everything and follows Jesus, like Peter, James, and John before him. In return, Levi holds a banquet for Jesus and invites other "tax collectors and sinners" in order to introduce them to Jesus. The fact that Jesus shares table fellowship with such undesirables makes the Pharisees and scribes question the nature of his mission and the type of "kingdom" he proclaims. Their separatism is a strong contrast to the inclusive outreach of Jesus. His mission, Jesus responds, is to heal the sick, not the healthy, and to care for the sinners, not the righteous. His goal for all people is repentance: recognizing their need for God, reorienting their life to the priorities of God, and seeking forgiveness and salvation through God's grace.

Reflection and discussion

• How does Jesus demonstrate that he gives more than a physical cure to the leper and the paralytic? What is the greater healing for each?

• Why is forgiveness the greatest healing? Do I believe that Jesus wants to heal me and make me whole?

• What does Jesus' choice of Levi teach me about Jesus? What does Levi's choice of guests teach me about being a Christian?

Prayer

Father of the outcasts, I cry out to you in my need. Divine Physician, restore the wholeness that I have lost through sin. I believe that you can heal me with your word and your touch. Help me to turn to you in repentance and trust in you.

Now during those days he went out to the mountain to pray; and he spent the night in prayer to God. And when day came, he called his disciples and chose twelve of them, whom he also named apostles. Luke 6:12-13

Controversies and Calling

LUKE 5:33–6:16 ³³*Then they said to him, "John's disciples, like the disciples of the Pharisees, frequently fast and pray, but your disciples eat and drink.* ³⁴*Jesus said to them, "You cannot make wedding guests fast while the bridegroom is with them, can you?* ³⁵*The days will come when the bridegroom will be taken away from them, and then they will fast in those days."* ³⁶*He also told them a parable: "No one tears a piece from a new garment and sews it on an old garment; otherwise the new will be torn, and the piece from the new will not match the old.* ³⁷*And no one puts new wine into old wineskins; otherwise the new wine will burst the skins and will be spilled, and the skins will be destroyed.* ³⁸*But new wine must be put into fresh wineskins.* ³⁹*And no one after drinking old wine desires new wine, but says, 'The old is good.'"*

6 ¹*One sabbath while Jesus was going through the grainfields, his disciples plucked some heads of grain, rubbed them in their hands, and ate them.* ²*But some of the Pharisees said, "Why are you doing what is not lawful on the sabbath?"* ³*Jesus answered, "Have you not read what David did when he and his companions were hungry?* ⁴*He entered the house of God and took and ate the bread of the Presence, which it is not lawful for any but the priests to eat, and gave some to his companions."* ⁵*Then he said to them, "The Son of Man is lord of the sabbath."*

⁶*On another sabbath he entered the synagogue and taught, and there was a man there whose right hand was withered. ⁷The scribes and the Pharisees watched him to see whether he would cure on the sabbath, so that they might find an accusation against him. ⁸Even though he knew what they were thinking, he said to the man who had the withered hand, "Come and stand here." He got up and stood there. ⁹Then Jesus said to them, "I ask you, is it lawful to do good or to do harm on the sabbath, to save life or to destroy it?" ¹⁰After looking around at all of them, he said to him, "Stretch out your hand." He did so, and his hand was restored. ¹¹But they were filled with fury and discussed with one another what they might do to Jesus.*

¹²*Now during those days he went out to the mountain to pray; and he spent the night in prayer to God. ¹³And when day came, he called his disciples and chose twelve of them, whom he also named apostles: ¹⁴Simon, whom he named Peter, and his brother Andrew, and James, and John, and Philip, and Bartholomew, ¹⁵and Matthew, and Thomas, and James son of Alphaeus, and Simon, who was called the Zealot, ¹⁶and Judas son of James, and Judas Iscariot, who became a traitor.*

The gospel presents us here with three controversies: the first emerges from a question about fasting and is followed by two accounts dealing with practices on the Sabbath. While it may seem that these controversies are primarily concerned with how disciples are to live with regard to the controversial practices of fasting and Sabbath regulations, they are really about who Jesus is and what he brings into the world. Through the first controversy, Jesus is shown to be the bridegroom, bringing joy and welcoming people to the wedding banquet. In the following, Jesus proclaims that he is lord of the Sabbath, the final fulfillment of God's gift of the Sabbath.

The extended metaphors offered by Jesus demonstrate that the kingdom that Jesus brings is a new way (verses 36-38). It is a new garment that cannot be used to repair an old garment, and it is new wine, which needs a new container for its expansion. Many of the old practices within Judaism do not fit into the new age of salvation that Jesus is bringing for all people.

Just as an old garment should never be patched with the material from a new garment, the gospel of God's kingdom cannot simply be a repair for the old ways of Judaism. The new cloth is ripped and does not match the old, so the good news of Jesus cannot be destroyed for the sake of the institutions of ancient Israel. Likewise, as new wine should never be stored in old, brittle wineskins, the gospel cannot be contained within the constraints of Judaism. The old wineskin bursts and the new wine is poured out, so the new message of the kingdom must not be lost, but must be contained within fresh, new ways of expressing what God is doing in Jesus.

Jesus warns that many in Judaism will likely reject the new way of salvation offered by Jesus. Those who are accustomed to the old wine, the narrow values of the religious authorities, will not even taste the new; for the old, they say, is good enough (verse 39). But the ways of God's kingdom, open to all people, cannot fit with the old ways and require new ways of thinking and acting according to the ways of God's kingdom. The Acts of the Apostles will demonstrate how these controversies are resolved as the early church refuses to require new believers in Jesus to practice the distinct ways of Judaism.

The first controversy contrasts the practices of the disciples of John the Baptist and the Pharisees with the practices of Jesus' disciples. The disciples of John "frequently fast and pray," while the disciples of Jesus "eat and drink." Jesus responds that fasting is inappropriate when the bridegroom has arrived and is calling his guests into the wedding banquet of the kingdom. Fasting is preparation; marriage is fulfillment. The second and third controversies concern the prescription of the Torah that no work should be done on the seventh day of the week, a law designed to protect the wholeness of human life. In Judaism, the Sabbath is a foretaste and preparation for God's kingdom. Since Jesus proclaims the good news of God's kingdom, it is inappropriate to restrict expressions of human wholeness and healing, which are signs of the kingdom. Satisfying the hunger of Jesus' disciples and curing the man with the withered hand are demonstrations that indeed the kingdom of God is at hand.

As those who oppose Jesus begin to organize (verse 11), Jesus begins to organize his disciples (verse 13). After spending the night in prayer to the Father, Jesus solemnly chooses twelve of his disciples in order to train them for leadership and mission. These twelve will be the nucleus of the restored and renewed Israel. As apostles, they will be the commissioned representatives of Jesus. They will be the first sent on mission, and from them almost all the major leaders of the church will be drawn.

Reflection and discussion

• How is Jesus like a bridegroom? How is the gospel Jesus proclaims like a new garment and new wine?

• If fasting is a way of preparing for a feast, why did the church return to the practice of fasting after the earthly life of Jesus?

• The multiple prohibitions contained in the Sabbath law are intended to make it a joyful delight. What does the tradition of Judaism teach me about the importance of laws and regulations in safeguarding religious traditions?

Prayer

Divine Bridegroom, you invite your followers to the wedding feast of God's kingdom. Give me a joyful and passionate desire to unite my life to you in discipleship. May I put on the new garment of your life and drink the new wine of the kingdom.

> "Rejoice in that day and leap for joy,
> for surely your reward is great in heaven;
> for that is what their ancestors did to the prophets." Luke 6:23

Reversing Expectations about Success and Failure

LUKE 6:17-26 *¹⁷He came down with them and stood on a level place, with a great crowd of his disciples and a great multitude of people from all Judea, Jerusalem, and the coast of Tyre and Sidon. ¹⁸They had come to hear him and to be healed of their diseases; and those who were troubled with unclean spirits were cured. ¹⁹And all in the crowd were trying to touch him, for power came out from him and healed all of them.*

²⁰Then he looked up at his disciples and said:

"Blessed are you who are poor,
* for yours is the kingdom of God.*
²¹"Blessed are you who are hungry now,
* for you will be filled.*
"Blessed are you who weep now,
* for you will laugh.*
²²"Blessed are you when people hate you, and when they exclude you, revile you, and defame you on account of the Son of Man. ²³Rejoice in that day and leap for joy, for surely your reward is great in heaven; for that is what their ancestors did to the prophets.

24 *"But woe to you who are rich,*
for you have received your consolation.
25 *"Woe to you who are full now,*
for you will be hungry.
"Woe to you who are laughing now,
for you will mourn and weep.
26 *"Woe to you when all speak well of you, for that is what*
their ancestors did to the false prophets.

After Jesus descends the mountain with his chosen twelve apostles, a great multitude gathers on a stretch of level ground. The crowd, from throughout the whole region of Palestine and from as far away as Tyre and Sidon, indicates the widening popular interest in Jesus. The multitude consists of disciples and a host of people who come to listen to Jesus teach and to be healed by him. Jesus compassionately ministers to them in word and deed, healing their diseases and releasing them from the evil forces that oppress them, before he turns to address his disciples.

This "sermon on the plain," as it is traditionally called, is similar to the "sermon on the mount" in Matthew's gospel (Matt 5–7). It sets out the basic ethical standards for those who choose to live within the community Jesus is establishing. As in Matthew's gospel, Jesus begins the sermon with beatitudes, placing his moral teachings within the context of God's blessings. Here, the passage divides into two parts: blessings (verses 20-23) and woes (verses 24-26). Jesus compares the blessed ones with the ancient prophets of Israel, while comparing the condemned to the false prophets. People are divided into two groupings: poor and rich, hungry and satisfied, humble and proud, responsive and unresponsive. The listeners are challenged to decide to which of the two camps they belong.

In contrast to the more generic standards of Matthew's beatitudes, the standards recorded here are directed to the immediate condition of the audience—those listening to Jesus and those reading the gospel. He addresses "you who are poor," "you who are now hungry," and "you who weep now." Declaring someone "blessed" is common throughout the Scriptures. The designation refers to a sense of inner happiness, good fortune, and peace.

Although the beatitudes are in the present tense, they have a future promise in view. Although the kingdom of God now belongs to the poor, hungry, weeping, and rejected, they will possess it fully later. As such, these beatitudes are expressions of hope that extend into the future. The promise is inaugurated here and how, but it will reach its total fulfillment for those who remain united and identified with Jesus.

The poor are those who are in desperate need, whose powerlessness drives them to depend on God. Yet, Jesus proclaims that the good news of the kingdom is theirs. The hungry are those who are painfully deficient in the things essential to life, yet Jesus proclaims that they will recline at table and share in the banquet of the kingdom. The poor and hungry are now weeping because they suffer from injustice, but the time will come when they will laugh with eternal joy.

Jesus knows that his disciples will be persecuted and rejected for their faith in him. Yet, it is their association with him in the present that unlocks the blessings. Their experience of being opposed, ostracized, insulted, and discarded will give way to blessings and reward. In fact, disciples of Jesus can rejoice in the midst of their suffering for him. God knows their suffering, and Jesus assures them that they will be honored for their faithfulness. This gladness in the middle of persecution and rejection is a characteristic of the church that Luke will demonstrate in the Acts of the Apostles.

The four woes form a contrast to the blessings. "Woe" is an exclamation of anguish and pity for the misfortune that awaits a person in a certain condition. In Scripture, the woes warn of danger and the nearness of God's judgment. Here they serve as a warning and a call to repentance for those who are tempted to trust too greatly in wealth, possessions, comfort, and fame.

The rich and famous are not excluded from God's kingdom as a class or socioeconomic group, because Jesus had wealthy and influential followers. Rather, he condemns their misplaced focus, the attitude they often display, and their lack of concern for God's desires and the needs of others. An attitude of self-sufficiency and autonomy from God leads to ultimate destruction. Its reward is fleeting and limited to the present.

Reflection and discussion

• Am I among the poor and hungry or the rich and satisfied? How blessed am I in the eyes of God?

• When have I experienced rejection or scorn because of my faith in Jesus Christ? Am I able to rejoice in the midst of these difficulties?

• In what ways do riches, power, and fame tend to make people spiritually insensitive?

Prayer

Father in heaven, your Son has instilled a love and longing for your king-dom in my heart. Give me the grace to live by the standards of your kingdom and to give to others with generosity and compassion.

"Can a blind person guide a blind person? Will not both fall into a pit?
A disciple is not above the teacher, but everyone who is fully qualified
will be like the teacher." Luke 6:39-40

Prophetic Teaching of Jesus

LUKE 6:27-49 [27]*"But I say to you that listen, Love your enemies, do good to
those who hate you,* [28]*bless those who curse you, pray for those who abuse you.*
[29]*If anyone strikes you on the cheek, offer the other also; and from anyone who
takes away your coat do not withhold even your shirt.* [30]*Give to everyone who
begs from you; and if anyone takes away your goods, do not ask for them again.*
[31]*Do to others as you would have them do to you.*

[32]*"If you love those who love you, what credit is that to you? For even sinners
love those who love them.* [33]*If you do good to those who do good to you, what
credit is that to you? For even sinners do the same.* [34]*If you lend to those from
whom you hope to receive, what credit is that to you? Even sinners lend to sinners, to receive as much again.* [35]*But love your enemies, do good, and lend,
expecting nothing in return. Your reward will be great, and you will be children
of the Most High; for he is kind to the ungrateful and the wicked.* [36]*Be merciful,
just as your Father is merciful.*

[37]*"Do not judge, and you will not be judged; do not condemn, and you will
not be condemned. Forgive, and you will be forgiven;* [38]*give, and it will be given
to you. A good measure, pressed down, shaken together, running over, will be
put into your lap; for the measure you give will be the measure you get back."*

[39]*He also told them a parable: "Can a blind person guide a blind person? Will*

not both fall into a pit? [40]*A disciple is not above the teacher, but everyone who is fully qualified will be like the teacher.* [41]*Why do you see the speck in your neighbor's eye, but do not notice the log in your own eye?* [42]*Or how can you say to your neighbor, 'Friend, let me take out the speck in your eye,' when you yourself do not see the log in your own eye? You hypocrite, first take the log out of your own eye, and then you will see clearly to take the speck out of your neighbor's eye.*

[43]*"No good tree bears bad fruit, nor again does a bad tree bear good fruit;* [44]*for each tree is known by its own fruit. Figs are not gathered from thorns, nor are grapes picked from a bramble bush.* [45]*The good person out of the good treasure of the heart produces good, and the evil person out of evil treasure produces evil; for it is out of the abundance of the heart that the mouth speaks.*

[46]*"Why do you call me 'Lord, Lord,' and do not do what I tell you?* [47]*I will show you what someone is like who comes to me, hears my words, and acts on them.* [48]*That one is like a man building a house, who dug deeply and laid the foundation on rock; when a flood arose, the river burst against that house but could not shake it, because it had been well built.* [49]*But the one who hears and does not act is like a man who built a house on the ground without a foundation. When the river burst against it, immediately it fell, and great was the ruin of that house."*

T he exhortations to love your enemies, do good to those who hate you, pray for those who mistreat you (verses 27-28), give generously to those who ask of you (verse 30), and lend without expecting anything in return (verse 34) greatly exceed human expectations. The standards Jesus sets are remarkably high, going far beyond the more accepted standards of doing for others what we would want done for us.

The ultimate standard for discipleship is to do what God would do: "Be merciful, just as your Father is merciful" (verse 36). To live in God's kingdom means loving as God loves, caring for others as God cares for them, giving as generously as God gives, forgiving others as God forgives. The generosity and compassion of God is the source and motivation for the ethical deeds of the new disciple of Jesus.

The prayer, good deeds, blessings, forgiveness, and generosity that Jesus urges upon his followers are all forms of Christian love. This merciful love is a response to the generosity, blessings, and forgiveness God has bestowed upon us. We can only love in this supernatural way because God has extended his grace upon us in such incredible abundance.

This love in imitation of God does not just respond in kind to the way people treat us; there is nothing new or radical about that. The ancient world often lived on the premise, "Do good to others so that they will do good to you." But Jesus' command has no hidden agenda; it is love for love's sake. Those who love in this way show themselves to be "children of the Most High," sons and daughters who take on the character of their Father and are rewarded with his favor (verse 35).

When we refuse to judge and condemn others, but rather forgive and show generosity, our own lives will be characterized by that kind of abundance. God is like a seller measuring grain in the marketplace. He fills the container, presses it down, gives it a good shake, then heaps the grain to overflowing while emptying the grain into the lap of the buyer. In this way, God pours abundance into our lives in an absolutely full and overflowing measure (verse 38).

The sermon concludes with a series of parabolic lessons in which Jesus challenges his disciples to take his words seriously and to examine their own lives in light of his teachings. The images are all in pairs: the teacher and disciple (verse 40), the speck in the neighbor's eye and the log in one's own eye (verse 41), the good and the bad tree (verse 43), the good and the evil person (verse 45), and the house that stands and the one that is washed away (verses 48-49). The illustrations each challenge the readers to make a choice, a choice that is not difficult once one sees what is at stake.

The proverb about the blind leading the blind demonstrates that a teacher needs clear vision before leading others in the way (verse 39). Before we can be qualified to help others, we must look at ourselves first. We have to remove the log in our own eye before we can focus on the speck in the eye of another. Of course, the speck and the log represent personal faults that are worthy of correction. Jesus urges his followers to be hesitant to judge and condemn others and quick to forgive and show mercy. When we see clearly, we are able to deal sensitively with others and serve them with both truth and compassion.

The images of the good and bad trees illustrate how the fruit that we produce in life reflects what is at the core of our being. Because figs and grapes do not come from thorns and brambles, we should take a careful look at our lives to see what kind of fruit we are bearing. The mouth speaks words that come from the treasure that lies in our heart. The words and deeds that we express indicate the spiritual condition of our lives.

In the final lesson of his sermon, Jesus teaches that a disciple is one who not only calls him "Lord," but also puts his teachings into practice (verse 46). By doing what he commands us, disciples make the lordship of Jesus a concrete, living reality. Jesus offers us the pattern for genuine discipleship: we must come to Jesus, listen to his words, and put those words into action. Such a person is like one who digs a deep and solid foundation for his home. A home built in this way will withstand any storm. Likewise, the genuine disciple will be able to stand strong in the face of the trials and opposition that are sure to come.

Reflection and discussion

• Why does Jesus urge us to pray for those who oppose us rather than seek revenge? What might be the result of that kind of intercession?

• How were these words of Jesus heard by the early church in the face of persecution? Are these teachings of Jesus realistic for today?

Prayer

Most High God, you are generous, merciful, and forgiving. Help me to live according to the teachings of Jesus so that my life will have a firm foundation and bear the fruit of compassionate service.

"Lord, do not trouble yourself, for I am not worthy to have you come under my roof; therefore I did not presume to come to you. But only speak the word, and let my servant be healed." Luke 7:6-7

The Healing Power of Jesus

LUKE 7:1-17 ¹*After Jesus had finished all his sayings in the hearing of the people, he entered Capernaum.* ²*A centurion there had a slave whom he valued highly, and who was ill and close to death.* ³*When he heard about Jesus, he sent some Jewish elders to him, asking him to come and heal his slave.* ⁴*When they came to Jesus, they appealed to him earnestly, saying, "He is worthy of having you do this for him,* ⁵*for he loves our people, and it is he who built our synagogue for us."* ⁶*And Jesus went with them, but when he was not far from the house, the centurion sent friends to say to him, "Lord, do not trouble yourself, for I am not worthy to have you come under my roof;* ⁷*therefore I did not presume to come to you. But only speak the word, and let my servant be healed.* ⁸*For I also am a man set under authority, with soldiers under me; and I say to one, 'Go,' and he goes, and to another, 'Come,' and he comes, and to my slave, 'Do this,' and the slave does it."* ⁹*When Jesus heard this he was amazed at him, and turning to the crowd that followed him, he said, "I tell you, not even in Israel have I found such faith."* ¹⁰*When those who had been sent returned to the house, they found the slave in good health.*

¹¹*Soon afterwards he went to a town called Nain, and his disciples and a large crowd went with him.* ¹²*As he approached the gate of the town, a man who had died was being carried out. He was his mother's only son, and she was a widow;*

and with her was a large crowd from the town. ¹³ *When the Lord saw her, he had compassion for her and said to her, "Do not weep."* ¹⁴ *Then he came forward and touched the bier, and the bearers stood still. And he said, "Young man, I say to you, rise!"* ¹⁵ *The dead man sat up and began to speak, and Jesus gave him to his mother.* ¹⁶ *Fear seized all of them; and they glorified God, saying, "A great prophet has risen among us!" and "God has looked favorably on his people!"* ¹⁷ *This word about him spread throughout Judea and all the surrounding country.*

I n these two accounts, the healing of the centurion's slave and the raising of the widow's son, Jesus shows himself to be like the great prophets of Israel, especially Elijah and Elisha. Indeed, the people rejoice that "a great prophet has arisen among us!" and through him "God has looked favorably on his people!" (verse 16). Later in the gospel the crowds marvel at the works of Jesus, and they think that "one of the ancient prophets has arisen" (9:19).

The healing of the centurion's servant resembles the account in 2 Kings 5:1-14 in which Naaman, a Gentile army commander, is cured by the prophet Elisha. The raising of the widow's son is similar to the account in 1 Kings 17:17-24 in which the prophet Elijah raises the dead son of the widow at Zarephath. In these two accounts, the words Jesus spoke at Nazareth about his own prophetic ministry are being fulfilled (4:25-27).

The focus of the first healing account is not the healing of the servant but the faith of the centurion. This Roman army officer must have been well known to the people of Capernaum since he built their synagogue, but as a Gentile, he is hesitant about asking a Jewish teacher for help. So he sends some Jewish elders to ask Jesus to come and heal the slave that the centurion so highly esteems.

These emissaries implore Jesus on the man's behalf by describing the centurion as "worthy" of having Jesus do this for him since he is sympathetic to the Jews (verse 4). This description of the centurion as "worthy" contrasts with his own evaluation of himself. When Jesus approaches his house, the centurion sends his friends to speak for him these words: "Lord, do not trouble yourself, for I am not worthy to have you come under my roof" (verse 6). He knows that God is working powerfully through Jesus and that the word of Jesus, spoken from afar, will heal his servant. Just as he is obeyed by his soldiers and slaves, the centurion trusts that those forces afflicting his dying servant will obey Jesus.

Jesus expresses amazement at the total and trusting faith of this Gentile officer. He holds him up to the crowds as a model. The centurion expresses a deep, personal humility, and he recognizes Jesus' authority and the power of his word, even in the face of physical absence and distance. Jesus commends the faith of the Gentile as something not found in Israel, foreshadowing the expansion of Jesus' ministry to the Gentiles of all nations. Racial and religious distinctions are of no consequence when one receives the gospel of Jesus Christ.

The second healing account occurs in the small Galilean town of Nain. When Jesus and his disciples approach the town, they observe a funeral procession in which a dead man is being carried outside the city gate to a burial place. Usually the burial occurred on the same day as the death, after the body was anointed, wrapped in cloth on a burial plank, and carried outside the city to the family cemetery. The note that the man was "his mother's only son, and she was a widow" shows that now she has no male family member to provide for her. Jesus takes the initiative and speaks a word of comfort to the weeping mother as he prepares to deal with her tragic situation.

As Jesus touches the plank where the anointed and shrouded corpse lay, the procession stops. Three simple statements describe Jesus' resuscitation of the young man (verses 14-15). First, with his word alone Jesus calls him to rise up; second, the dead man returns to life, sits up, and speaks; and third, Jesus gives him back to his mother, restoring the relationship broken by death. The response of the crowd is described in two ways: a respectful awe fell upon them and they gave glory to God by honoring Jesus. In calling Jesus a great prophet, they realize how his works parallel yet surpass the works of Elijah and Elisha. The outsiders and the defenseless can experience in Jesus the invitation to experience God's renewed favor.

Reflection and discussion

• On what basis do the Jewish elders request Jesus' help for the centurion? How does their approach differ from the way the centurion approaches Jesus?

• Why would the account of Jesus' healing of the centurion's servant be particularly helpful for the readers of Luke's gospel in the first-century church? What does it teach me in the twenty-first-century church?

How do these two miracles express the fact that the ministry of Jesus surpasses and completes the work of Elijah and Elisha?

• What does the account of the healing of the widow's son teach me about Jesus?

Prayer

Merciful Lord, I am not worthy that you should enter under my roof. I ask you to have compassion on me in my need as I have confidence in your authority. Speak only the word and my soul shall be healed.

"Go and tell John what you have seen and heard: the blind receive
their sight, the lame walk, the lepers are cleansed, the deaf hear,
the dead are raised, the poor have good news brought to them." Luke 7:22

The One Who Is To Come

LUKE 7:18-50 [18]*The disciples of John reported all these things to him. So
John summoned two of his disciples* [19]*and sent them to the Lord to ask, "Are you
the one who is to come, or are we to wait for another?"* [20]*When the men had
come to him, they said, "John the Baptist has sent us to you to ask, 'Are you the
one who is to come, or are we to wait for another?'"* [21]*Jesus had just then cured
many people of diseases, plagues, and evil spirits, and had given sight to many
who were blind.* [22]*And he answered them, "Go and tell John what you have seen
and heard: the blind receive their sight, the lame walk, the lepers are cleansed,
the deaf hear, the dead are raised, the poor have good news brought to them.*
[23]*And blessed is anyone who takes no offense at me."*

[24]*When John's messengers had gone, Jesus began to speak to the crowds about
John: "What did you go out into the wilderness to look at? A reed shaken by the
wind?* [25]*What then did you go out to see? Someone dressed in soft robes? Look,
those who put on fine clothing and live in luxury are in royal palaces.* [26]*What
then did you go out to see? A prophet? Yes, I tell you, and more than a prophet.*
[27]*This is the one about whom it is written,*

   'See, I am sending my messenger ahead of you,

     who will prepare your way before you.'

[28]*I tell you, among those born of women no one is greater than John; yet the
least in the kingdom of God is greater than he."* [29]*(And all the people who heard*

this, including the tax collectors, acknowledged the justice of God, because they had been baptized with John's baptism. [30]*But by refusing to be baptized by him, the Pharisees and the lawyers rejected God's purpose for themselves.)*

[31]*"To what then will I compare the people of this generation, and what are they like?* [32]*They are like children sitting in the marketplace and calling to one another,*

'*We played the flute for you, and you did not dance;*

we wailed, and you did not weep.'

[33]*"For John the Baptist has come eating no bread and drinking no wine, and you say, 'He has a demon';* [34]*the Son of Man has come eating and drinking, and you say, 'Look, a glutton and a drunkard, a friend of tax collectors and sinners!'* [35]*Nevertheless, wisdom is vindicated by all her children."*

[36]*One of the Pharisees asked Jesus to eat with him, and he went into the Pharisee's house and took his place at the table.* [37]*And a woman in the city, who was a sinner, having learned that he was eating in the Pharisee's house, brought an alabaster jar of ointment.* [38]*She stood behind him at his feet, weeping, and began to bathe his feet with her tears and to dry them with her hair. Then she continued kissing his feet and anointing them with the ointment.* [39]*Now when the Pharisee who had invited him saw it, he said to himself, "If this man were a prophet, he would have known who and what kind of woman this is who is touching him—that she is a sinner."* [40]*Jesus spoke up and said to him, "Simon, I have something to say to you." "Teacher," he replied, "speak."* [41]*"A certain creditor had two debtors; one owed five hundred denarii, and the other fifty.* [42]*When they could not pay, he canceled the debts for both of them. Now which of them will love him more?"* [43]*Simon answered, "I suppose the one for whom he canceled the greater debt." And Jesus said to him, "You have judged rightly."* [44]*Then turning toward the woman, he said to Simon, "Do you see this woman? I entered your house; you gave me no water for my feet, but she has bathed my feet with her tears and dried them with her hair.* [45]*You gave me no kiss, but from the time I came in she has not stopped kissing my feet.* [46]*You did not anoint my head with oil, but she has anointed my feet with ointment.* [47]*Therefore, I tell you, her sins, which were many, have been forgiven; hence she has shown great love. But the one to whom little is forgiven, loves little."* [48]*Then he said to her, "Your sins are forgiven."* [49]*But those who were at the table with him began to say among themselves, "Who is this who even forgives sins?"* [50]*And he said to the woman, "Your faith has saved you; go in peace."*

Through his disciples, John the Baptist asks if Jesus is "the one who is to come" (verses 19-20). The response of Jesus reassures John, as well as all of us who read Luke's gospel, that he truly is the one. The evidence is provided by the deeds of Jesus: he heals and restores wholeness to the blind, the lame, the lepers, the deaf, and even the dead; and he proclaims good news to the poor. Those things that Isaiah associated with the era of salvation are the very things that Jesus is doing (see Isa 29:18-19; 35:5-6; 61:1). He is not just a great prophet, but he is the coming Messiah.

It is remarkable that John the Baptist did not know whether or not Jesus was the one for whom he had prepared the way. During his ministry John had proclaimed Jesus as the one coming as a mighty deliverer, reformer, and judge. According to John, the coming one would carry a winnowing fork of judgment, ready to gather in the wheat and burn the chaff. Yet, Jesus came as an instrument of God's mercy to the sinner, the sick, and the dead. Like John and the people of Jesus' day, we too have preconceived ideas of who Jesus should be. If even John failed to understand Jesus fully, we too can expect to struggle as we seek to know him better.

John the Baptist is the bridge figure in the transition from the age of promise to the era of fulfillment. He is the last of the great prophets sent to prepare the way for the coming of the Messiah (verse 27)—indeed, according to Jesus, he is the greatest person who has ever lived up to this point (verse 28). Yet, now the age of God's kingdom has begun, and all those called to the kingdom are invited into an abundance of life that could only be imagined by John and those who lived before him.

Simon the Pharisee, like John the Baptist, fails to understand Jesus. Simon assumes that if Jesus really is a prophet, he will draw away from the woman kissing his feet, because she is a sinner (verse 39). Jesus did not meet Simon's expectations because he did not withdraw from the woman, but assured her of God's forgiveness, nor did Jesus meet John's expectations because he was a minister of mercy rather than of judgment. The misunderstanding of both John and Simon demonstrates the way that God continues to reverse human expectations in the works of Jesus.

The account presents a contrast between Simon the Pharisee and the woman. Simon is not moved by Jesus' presence in his home. He does not offer Jesus the signs of hospitality: washing his feet, greeting him with a kiss, and anointing him with oil (verses 44-46). The woman, on the other hand, is extravagant in her displays of love because she has received forgiveness (verse 47). Simon is like the debtor who has been forgiven a smaller amount because he is less willing to acknowledge his sins (verses 41-42). Thus, Simon was unable to love as lavishly as the woman.

The woman's extravagant acts of love teach us that forgiveness allows us to love. The more we recognize our sinfulness and ask for God's forgiveness, the more we can receive God's mercy and demonstrate love for others. The love that Jesus shows us in offering us forgiveness gives us the motivation and grace to love without counting the costs. When we accept the gift of forgiveness, we can love generously and lavishly.

Reflection and discussion

• What preconceived ideas do I have about Jesus that the gospel is showing as inaccurate or too narrow? Do I fail to recognize the presence of Jesus in the world because my expectations of him are inadequate?

• Do I measure out my love, or do I love extravagantly? When has God's forgiveness freed me to love generously?

Prayer

Merciful God, have mercy on me, a sinner. Help me to trust in your power to forgive so that I may love as you love. Let me experience healing and wholeness as you draw me into your kingdom to experience life in abundance.

SUGGESTIONS FOR FACILITATORS, GROUP SESSION 4

1. Welcome group members and ask if anyone has any questions, announcements, or requests.

2. You may want to pray this prayer as a group:

Father, your Son is known as a friend of tax collectors and sinners, the great physician, the bridegroom who calls us to the wedding banquet, the Lord of the Sabbath, and the one who is to come. As we continue to deepen our understanding of his identity, continue calling us to faith and repentance as we respond to his invitation to discipleship. As we witness the ministry of Jesus to the leper, the paralytic, the centurion's servant, the widow's son, and the sinful woman, may he continue to make us whole and call us to the abundance of your kingdom.

3. Ask one or more of the following questions:
   - What is the most difficult part of this study for you?
   - What insights stand out to you from the lessons this week?

4. Discuss lessons 13 through 18. Choose one or more of the questions for reflection and discussion from each lesson to discuss as a group. You may want to ask group members which question was most challenging or helpful to them as you review each lesson.

5. Keep the discussion moving, but allow time for the questions that provoke the most discussion. Encourage the group members to use "I" language in their responses.

6. After talking over each lesson, instruct group members to complete lessons 19 through 24 on their own during the six days before the next group meeting. They should write out their own answers to the questions as preparation for next week's session.

7. Ask the group what encouragement they need for the coming week. Ask the members to pray for the needs of one another during the week.

8. Conclude by praying aloud together the prayer at the end of one of the lessons discussed. You may choose to conclude the prayer by asking members to pray aloud any requests they may have.

"But as for that in the good soil, these are the ones who, when they hear the word, hold it fast in an honest and good heart, and bear fruit with patient endurance." Luke 8:15

Hearing and Doing the Word of God

LUKE 8:1-21 ¹*Soon afterwards he went on through cities and villages, proclaiming and bringing the good news of the kingdom of God. The twelve were with him, ²as well as some women who had been cured of evil spirits and infirmities: Mary, called Magdalene, from whom seven demons had gone out, ³and Joanna, the wife of Herod's steward Chuza, and Susanna, and many others, who provided for them out of their resources.*

⁴When a great crowd gathered and people from town after town came to him, he said in a parable: ⁵"A sower went out to sow his seed; and as he sowed, some fell on the path and was trampled on, and the birds of the air ate it up. ⁶Some fell on the rock; and as it grew up, it withered for lack of moisture. ⁷Some fell among thorns, and the thorns grew with it and choked it. ⁸Some fell into good soil, and when it grew, it produced a hundredfold." As he said this, he called out, "Let anyone with ears to hear listen!"

⁹Then his disciples asked him what this parable meant. ¹⁰He said, "To you it has been given to know the secrets of the kingdom of God; but to others I speak in parables, so that

'looking they may not perceive,

and listening they may not understand.'
[11]*"Now the parable is this: The seed is the word of God.* [12]*The ones on the path are those who have heard; then the devil comes and takes away the word from their hearts, so that they may not believe and be saved.* [13]*The ones on the rock are those who, when they hear the word, receive it with joy. But these have no root; they believe only for a while and in a time of testing fall away.* [14]*As for what fell among the thorns, these are the ones who hear; but as they go on their way, they are choked by the cares and riches and pleasures of life, and their fruit does not mature.* [15]*But as for that in the good soil, these are the ones who, when they hear the word, hold it fast in an honest and good heart, and bear fruit with patient endurance.*

[16]*"No one after lighting a lamp hides it under a jar, or puts it under a bed, but puts it on a lampstand, so that those who enter may see the light.* [17]*For nothing is hidden that will not be disclosed, nor is anything secret that will not become known and come to light.* [18]*Then pay attention to how you listen; for to those who have, more will be given; and from those who do not have, even what they seem to have will be taken away."*

[19]*Then his mother and his brothers came to him, but they could not reach him because of the crowd.* [20]*And he was told, "Your mother and your brothers are standing outside, wanting to see you."* [21]*But he said to them, "My mother and my brothers are those who hear the word of God and do it."*

Jesus did not proclaim the kingdom in isolation but traveled with companions. In addition to the Twelve, a group of women traveled with him and supported his ministry. Material support from women for an itinerant teacher was common at the time, but it was unusual for women to actually travel with the teacher.

Luke singles out three of these women for specific mention. Mary Magdalene was freed by Jesus from the presence of seven demons, and she responded by serving him. Joanna was the wife of an administrator in Herod's court; this indicates the reach of Jesus' ministry into influential circles. Susanna is mentioned only here, and the other women who traveled with Jesus remain unnamed.

The parable of the sower presents a farmer carrying a bag of grain over his shoulder and tossing the seed into the field. Some of the seed, however, falls on the well-beaten path over which travelers pass, so it is trampled on and eaten by birds. Some seed also falls in those parts of the field where a thin layer of soil covers limestone. Here the seed spouts, but the plants soon wither because the rocky ground cannot hold moisture. Other seed falls in ground where it must share the nutrients with thorny weeds. The plants grow, but they do not thrive and bear fruit. And other seed falls into good soil where it grows, produces fruit, and bears more seed.

After telling the parable, Jesus urges his hearers to "listen," insisting on the importance of reflecting on the teaching and responding to its message (verse 8). When the disciples ask for an explanation, Jesus tells them that the mysteries of God's kingdom are given to them by means of these parabolic instructions. Because they are committed to Jesus, the disciples better understand what God is doing through Jesus and receive insights through the parables. But to those who reject faith in Jesus, the parables are incomprehensible and conceal what God is doing.

As he explains the parable, Jesus makes the point that each group of people "hears" the word of God (verses 12-15). But it is how one responds to the hearing that makes all the difference. He warns, "Pay attention to how you listen" (verse 18). Only those who "believe" the word they have heard are "saved" (verse 12). To "believe" the word of God is not just a momentary choice; it is an ongoing, daily decision. Such faith does not vanish in times of testing (verse 12); it does not fade away when the initial enthusiasm for the good news disappears (verse 13); it does not die when crowded by the daily concerns of life (verse 14). Genuine faith in God's word matures and produces fruit when it is characterized by devotion and perseverance (verse 15).

Following the parable of the seed, Jesus offers the image of the lit lamp. The purpose of Jesus' teaching is to illumine the truth about God. Again, how one receives the word of God is absolutely crucial. The light is sometimes hidden for the same reasons that a seed fails to grow and thrive. It is essential to put the light on a lampstand where it will illumine its environment, because everything will eventually come to light and be disclosed. Our response to God's word reveals where our heart lies. For those who receive the light, responding positively to Jesus and his teachings, more blessings will follow. But those who hide the light of God's word eventually lose everything they possess.

The family of Jesus, then, consists of "those who hear the word of God and do it" (verse 21). This is not a repudiation of Jesus' natural family, because Mary herself is shown in Luke's writing to be the ideal disciple. But in the priorities of Jesus, the bonds of faith are superior to the ties of blood. His brothers and sister are those who allow his truth to shine, who nurture the word of God and allow it to bear fruit in the world. The reader of Luke's gospel is left with a choice. Will he or she be a member of the family?

Reflection and discussion

• What obstacles prevent me from hearing, believing, and doing the word of God?

• How can I prepare the soil of my life so that the word of God can take root and bear fruit?

• What does it mean to "hear the word of God and do it"? What fruit will the seed of God's word bear today through me?

Prayer

Lord God, you form your people by instilling the seed of your word within them. Help me to embrace your word with a generous heart and to bear fruit for your kingdom through my perseverance.

He woke up and rebuked the wind and the raging waves;
they ceased, and there was a calm. Luke 8:24

Authority over Storms and Demons

LUKE 8:22-39 *²²One day he got into a boat with his disciples, and he said to them, "Let us go across to the other side of the lake." So they put out, ²³and while they were sailing he fell asleep. A windstorm swept down on the lake, and the boat was filling with water, and they were in danger. ²⁴They went to him and woke him up, shouting, "Master, Master, we are perishing!" And he woke up and rebuked the wind and the raging waves; they ceased, and there was a calm. ²⁵He said to them, "Where is your faith?" They were afraid and amazed, and said to one another, "Who then is this, that he commands even the winds and the water, and they obey him?"*

²⁶Then they arrived at the country of the Gerasenes, which is opposite Galilee. ²⁷As he stepped out on land, a man of the city who had demons met him. For a long time he had worn no clothes, and he did not live in a house but in the tombs. ²⁸When he saw Jesus, he fell down before him and shouted at the top of his voice, "What have you to do with me, Jesus, Son of the Most High God? I beg you, do not torment me"—²⁹for Jesus had commanded the unclean spirit to come out of the man. (For many times it had seized him; he was kept under guard and bound with chains and shackles, but he would break the bonds and be driven by the demon into the wilds.) ³⁰Jesus then asked him, "What is your name?" He said, "Legion"; for many demons had entered him. ³¹They begged him not to order them to go back into the abyss.

³²Now there on the hillside a large herd of swine was feeding; and the demons begged Jesus to let them enter these. So he gave them permission. ³³Then the demons came out of the man and entered the swine, and the herd rushed down the steep bank into the lake and was drowned.

³⁴When the swineherds saw what had happened, they ran off and told it in the city and in the country. ³⁵Then people came out to see what had happened, and when they came to Jesus, they found the man from whom the demons had gone sitting at the feet of Jesus, clothed and in his right mind. And they were afraid. ³⁶Those who had seen it told them how the one who had been possessed by demons had been healed. ³⁷Then all the people of the surrounding country of the Gerasenes asked Jesus to leave them; for they were seized with great fear. So he got into the boat and returned. ³⁸The man from whom the demons had gone begged that he might be with him; but Jesus sent him away, saying, ³⁹"Return to your home, and declare how much God has done for you." So he went away, proclaiming throughout the city how much Jesus had done for him.

The Sea of Galilee is the site of frequent storms that can sweep down quickly, producing severe winds, large waves, and choppy waters. As the disciples are sailing the vessel, the boat is filling with water and they fear for their lives. In contrast to the raging storm, Jesus is sleeping peacefully in the boat. Panicked and desperate, the disciples awaken Jesus and shout, "Master, Master, we are perishing!" (verse 24). A situation that seems fraught with danger for the disciples is no cause for worry with Jesus. He immediately "rebuked" the wind and the waves, and brought about calm. This is the same verb previously used to describe Jesus' rebuke of an unclean spirit and the fever that accompanies disease (4:35, 39). Jesus can rebuke any powers hostile to people, whether it be evil spirits, disease, or natural force.

At one level of meaning, this account challenges the disciples to deeper faith and to a fuller understanding of Jesus. In the literature of Israel, God is the one who delivers his people from peril in the sea. When the disciples ask, "Who then is this, that he commands even the winds and the water, and they obey him?" we realize that Jesus' actions manifest divine power and protection. At another level of meaning, this account expresses the movement of the

Christian mission. The voyage of Jesus and his disciples "to the other side of the lake" is a journey from the Jewish lands to the Gentile territory (verses 22, 26). The journey represents the movement of the early church from the Jewish to the Gentile world, as Luke recounts in the Acts of the Apostles. The boat on the perilous sea is an early Christian symbol for the church. When the movement to the Gentiles created a period of turmoil for the early church and Jesus seemed to be absent or asleep, the disciples learned that they could trust in Jesus to bring calm and direction. Jesus asks his church and each of us the same question he asks his disciples in the boat, "Where is your faith?" (verse 25). As the church travels through rough passages and difficult transitions, we must believe that the Master is with us to deliver us from peril.

When Jesus and his disciples arrive on the other side of the Sea of Galilee, in the country of the Gerasenes, Jesus again demonstrates his power to control the forces that often overwhelm people. The demon-possessed man demonstrates the terrifying and destructive forces of evil at work within him. Yet, the legion of demons within him respect Jesus, knowing that he has divine authority and can do battle with them. So they beg Jesus to leave them alone and not torture them (verse 28). Fearing confinement in the abyss, the depths of the earth, they beg Jesus to let them enter a herd of swine on the hillside. When Jesus gives his permission, he relieves the man of his tormentors, but the time has not yet come when Jesus will deal with the powers of evil in a final or ultimate way by confining them to the abyss.

When the people of the area came to see what had happened, they observe the man in a complete reversal of his previous demeanor. He is clothed rather than naked, sitting at the feet of Jesus rather than roaming the hillside tombs, and in his right mind rather than shouting (verse 35). As the account ends, the changed man begs to go with Jesus, but Jesus sends him back to his home to declare how much God has done for him. The reply of Jesus tells us that some believers are called to travel with Jesus away from their home, while others are called to remain in their own locale and testify to the good news where they are.

The delivery of this man from the oppression of evil in the territory of the Gentiles shows that the ministry of Jesus goes beyond Israel, and it previews how the gospel is destined for all humanity. Jesus tells this new disciple to stay where he is among the Gentiles and to deliver the good news there. The man follows through on Jesus' commission and becomes an evangelizer, proclaiming the gospel throughout the city. Those who have been touched by the transforming ministry of Jesus cannot help but communicate that news to others.

Reflection and discussion

• What do these two miraculous stories have in common? Why did Luke choose to place them together?

• Why does Jesus sometimes deliver people through trials rather than from trials?

• Why are all disciples called to be evangelizers? What does it mean to communicate the good news to others?

Prayer

Master of storm and evil spirits, save me when I feel overwhelmed and insecure. When you seem to be asleep or seem to have abandoned me, let me cry out to you with confidence in your power to deliver me from harm.

Someone came from the leader's house to say, "Your daughter is dead;
do not trouble the teacher any longer." When Jesus heard this, he replied,
"Do not fear. Only believe, and she will be saved." Luke 8:49-50

Authority over Disease and Death

LUKE 8:40-56 [40]*Now when Jesus returned, the crowd welcomed him, for they were all waiting for him.* [41]*Just then there came a man named Jairus, a leader of the synagogue. He fell at Jesus' feet and begged him to come to his house,* [42]*for he had an only daughter, about twelve years old, who was dying.*

As he went, the crowds pressed in on him. [43]*Now there was a woman who had been suffering from hemorrhages for twelve years; and though she had spent all she had on physicians, no one could cure her.* [44]*She came up behind him and touched the fringe of his clothes, and immediately her hemorrhage stopped.* [45]*Then Jesus asked, "Who touched me?" When all denied it, Peter said, "Master, the crowds surround you and press in on you."* [46]*But Jesus said, "Someone touched me; for I noticed that power had gone out from me."* [47]*When the woman saw that she could not remain hidden, she came trembling; and falling down before him, she declared in the presence of all the people why she had touched him, and how she had been immediately healed.* [48]*He said to her, "Daughter, your faith has made you well; go in peace."*

[49]*While he was still speaking, someone came from the leader's house to say, "Your daughter is dead; do not trouble the teacher any longer."* [50]*When Jesus*

heard this, he replied, "Do not fear. Only believe, and she will be saved." ⁵¹*When he came to the house, he did not allow anyone to enter with him, except Peter, John, and James, and the child's father and mother.* ⁵²*They were all weeping and wailing for her; but he said, "Do not weep; for she is not dead but sleeping."* ⁵³*And they laughed at him, knowing that she was dead.* ⁵⁴*But he took her by the hand and called out, "Child, get up!"* ⁵⁵*Her spirit returned, and she got up at once. Then he directed them to give her something to eat.* ⁵⁶*Her parents were astounded; but he ordered them to tell no one what had happened.*

T he intertwined stories of these two "daughters" (verses 42, 48) are linked together by several elements. The girl is twelve years old (verse 42); the woman has had a flow of blood for twelve years (verse 43). The girl has enjoyed twelve years of advantage as the daughter of an honored synagogue ruler, while the woman has suffered twelve years of destitution. The girl is at the age when life seems full of possibilities, with a future of marriage and having children of her own. The woman has been prevented from the joys of marriage and childbirth because of her isolating condition. Both of their circumstances seem hopeless: the woman has not received a cure despite years of effort; the girl is on the verge of death and will soon die.

These two "daughters," isolated by sickness, desperation, and death, are saved by faith. Despite her debilitating condition, the woman with the hemorrhages approaches Jesus with courage and hope. She believes that if she can only touch the fringe of his clothes, she will be healed. When Jesus realizes that power has gone out from him and that the woman has been healed, he calls to her and says, "Daughter, your faith has made you well." Jairus is an influential leader of the synagogue, yet he approaches Jesus as a desperate parent, pleading for him to lay his healing hands on his daughter. When the news is brought of his daughter's death, Jesus urges him, "Do not fear. Only believe, and she will be saved" (verse 50). The faith of the woman and the faith of the girl's father brought them healing, life, and peace. Through these miracles, Jesus assures us that faith saves, that confident belief in his authority can bring us salvation and the fullness of life.

Both of these accounts are told in ways that encourage readers to have courage and confidence in the power of Jesus and to take initiative in seeking out his compassion. The afflicted woman seeks out Jesus and is persistent in her efforts to get to Jesus despite the many obstacles in her way. Though it is divine power in Jesus that cures her, she has to access that healing power for herself. Jesus praises her bold and assertive action, affirming the critical role of her own faith in securing her healing. Likewise, Jairus relinquishes his status as a religious leader and falls at the feet of Jesus, begging for his help. Even when his daughter has died, Jairus continues to trust and follows the instructions of Jesus. Although we know that the saving power of Jesus is always available to us, we must each engage his presence with confident and persistent faith.

These two intertwined accounts complete an escalating review of Jesus' comprehensive authority over all the forces that oppress us. He has authority over nature, demons, disease, and even death. Each of these accounts is part of Jesus' revelation to his disciples and helps answer the overarching question of this large section of Luke's gospel: Who is Jesus? In each account, Jesus acts with compassion toward a wide range of people: his disciples, a possessed Gentile, a synagogue leader, a child, and a suffering woman. Whether one is male or female, adult or child, Gentile or Jew, anonymous or at the center of influence, makes no difference to Jesus.

Reflection and discussion

• Why are these two healing accounts intertwined? What do these interwoven accounts together teach me about Jesus?

• In what ways does the story of the afflicted woman inspire me with courage, persistence, and trust?

• What is the reaction of Jesus to the news that Jairus' daughter had died? In what situations do I need to hear the words of Jesus, "Do not fear; only believe"?

• In what way does the faith of the people in these accounts lead me to a deeper faith?

Prayer

Father, your daughters and sons cry out to you with confident faith in your power to save. Help me to trust in your compassion so that I can respond to the ways you desire to work in my life. Free me from isolation, heal my infirmities, banish my doubts, and call me to life in its fullness.

Jesus called the twelve together and gave them power and authority over all demons and to cure diseases, and he sent them out to proclaim the kingdom of God and to heal. Luke 9:1-2

The Authority of the Apostles

LUKE 9:1-17 ¹*Then Jesus called the twelve together and gave them power and authority over all demons and to cure diseases, ²and he sent them out to proclaim the kingdom of God and to heal. ³He said to them, "Take nothing for your journey, no staff, nor bag, nor bread, nor money—not even an extra tunic. ⁴Whatever house you enter, stay there, and leave from there. ⁵Wherever they do not welcome you, as you are leaving that town shake the dust off your feet as a testimony against them." ⁶They departed and went through the villages, bringing the good news and curing diseases everywhere.*

⁷Now Herod the ruler heard about all that had taken place, and he was perplexed, because it was said by some that John had been raised from the dead, ⁸by some that Elijah had appeared, and by others that one of the ancient prophets had arisen. ⁹Herod said, "John I beheaded; but who is this about whom I hear such things?" And he tried to see him.

¹⁰On their return the apostles told Jesus all they had done. He took them with him and withdrew privately to a city called Bethsaida. ¹¹When the crowds found out about it, they followed him; and he welcomed them, and spoke to them about the kingdom of God, and healed those who needed to be cured.

¹²*The day was drawing to a close, and the twelve came to him and said, "Send the crowd away, so that they may go into the surrounding villages and country-side, to lodge and get provisions; for we are here in a deserted place."* ¹³*But he said to them, "You give them something to eat." They said, "We have no more than five loaves and two fish—unless we are to go and buy food for all these people."* ¹⁴*For there were about five thousand men. And he said to his disciples, "Make them sit down in groups of about fifty each."* ¹⁵*They did so and made them all sit down.* ¹⁶*And taking the five loaves and the two fish, he looked up to heaven, and blessed and broke them, and gave them to the disciples to set before the crowd.* ¹⁷*And all ate and were filled. What was left over was gathered up, twelve baskets of broken pieces.*

After the Twelve witness an impressive series of Jesus' teachings and healings, Jesus sends them out. This begins the active ministry on the part of those who have been following Jesus. The commission makes it clear that they are to do what Jesus does: "to proclaim the kingdom of God and to heal." Their power and authority is like that of Jesus, yet it is unmistakably derived from him. Through the Twelve, the gospel goes out to ever-larger circles.

Jesus tells them to travel light. Their lack of provisions demands that they depend on God for their every need and on the generosity of people who receive their message. The command to shake the dust from their feet when they leave a town that has not welcomed them is both a warning to their listeners about the seriousness of rejecting the gospel and also an acknowledgment that the disciples are not responsible for the choice made by their hearers. Faith in the gospel is a divine gift that must be freely received by the one to whom it is offered. No amount of persuasion can coerce a person to faith. Ministers are not at fault when people reject their proclamation of the kingdom.

Many messages about the identity of Jesus have circulated throughout Palestine: some said John had come back from the dead, others that Elijah or one of the ancient prophets had appeared. Word about Jesus has even reached the palace of Herod and is getting attention there. Those in the highest positions must also discern the identity of Jesus. Herod's question, "Who is this about whom I hear such things?" expresses the curiosity that Luke wants his readers to also share. Like so many others, Herod is trying to sort out who Jesus is, and so he desires to meet him.

As the Twelve return from their first mission, Jesus withdraws with them, perhaps for some solitary relaxation and time for debriefing their experience. Yet, as often happens when Jesus seeks time alone, the crowds find out his location, and Jesus continues his preaching and healing ministry. When evening comes and the Twelve urge Jesus to send the crowd away, he decides to teach them a lesson in shared ministry. Jesus dismisses their suggestion that he send the crowds away to look for food, and instead he says, "You give them something to eat" (verse 13).

When the Twelve protest that they have only five loaves and two fish for a crowd of thousands, Jesus gives them instructions to assemble the crowds in small groups for the distribution. Jesus then takes the food, implores heaven, blesses and breaks the food, and gives it to the disciples to set before the crowds. Jesus provides the food, but the disciples distribute it. Jesus feeds the people through the mediation of his disciples. In this way, Jesus not only teaches and feeds the crowd, but he offers his disciples a lesson in how they themselves can provide for the needs of God's people.

Even to the gathering of leftovers in twelve baskets, the Twelve learn to serve as ministers and delegates of Jesus. They, who will assume in Acts the role as leaders of the church, now begin to function as Jesus' representatives. They will continue to do what Jesus did, with his own power and authority. It will be their ongoing responsibility to nourish a hungry church. There are always sick who need healing, hungry people who need feeding, lost people who need the good news of God's kingdom.

Reflection and discussion

• What do Jesus' words about traveling light and shaking off the dust say to me about the mission of bringing faith to my family and neighbors?

• What are the differences between the way that Jesus and his disciples view the situation in verses 12 and 13?

• With five loaves and two fish, or whatever we have to give, we can ask and expect Jesus to multiply it for the needs of his people. When have I seen Jesus multiply the human efforts of his church into superabundant gifts?

• How have I experienced God's power working through my weakness? When has Jesus empowered me to do something for him that was beyond my ability?

Prayer

Lord God, you send out your people to continue the work of Jesus today. Give me what I need to proclaim, to heal, and to nourish, and help me trust in your Son's power to multiply my efforts for the sake of your kingdom.

> "If any want to become my followers, let them deny themselves
> and take up their cross daily and follow me.
> For those who want to save their life will lose it,
> and those who lose their life for my sake will save it." Luke 9:23-24

The Cost of Following Jesus

LUKE 9:18-36 [18]*Once when Jesus was praying alone, with only the disciples near him, he asked them, "Who do the crowds say that I am?"* [19]*They answered, "John the Baptist; but others, Elijah; and still others, that one of the ancient prophets has arisen."* [20]*He said to them, "But who do you say that I am?" Peter answered, "The Messiah of God."*

[21]*He sternly ordered and commanded them not to tell anyone,* [22]*saying, "The Son of Man must undergo great suffering, and be rejected by the elders, chief priests, and scribes, and be killed, and on the third day be raised."*

[23]*Then he said to them all, "If any want to become my followers, let them deny themselves and take up their cross daily and follow me.* [24]*For those who want to save their life will lose it, and those who lose their life for my sake will save it.* [25]*What does it profit them if they gain the whole world, but lose or forfeit themselves?* [26]*Those who are ashamed of me and of my words, of them the Son of Man will be ashamed when he comes in his glory and the glory of the Father and of the holy angels.* [27]*But truly I tell you, there are some standing here who will not taste death before they see the kingdom of God."*

[28]*Now about eight days after these sayings Jesus took with him Peter and John and James, and went up on the mountain to pray.* [29]*And while he was praying,*

the appearance of his face changed, and his clothes became dazzling white.
³⁰Suddenly they saw two men, Moses and Elijah, talking to him. ³¹They appeared
in glory and were speaking of his departure, which he was about to accomplish
at Jerusalem. ³²Now Peter and his companions were weighed down with sleep;
but since they had stayed awake, they saw his glory and the two men who stood
with him. ³³Just as they were leaving him, Peter said to Jesus, "Master, it is good
for us to be here; let us make three dwellings, one for you, one for Moses, and one
for Elijah" —not knowing what he said. ³⁴While he was saying this, a cloud came
and overshadowed them; and they were terrified as they entered the cloud.
³⁵Then from the cloud came a voice that said, "This is my Son, my Chosen; listen
to him!" ³⁶When the voice had spoken, Jesus was found alone. And they kept
silent and in those days told no one any of the things they had seen.

U p to this point in Luke's gospel, the accounts of Jesus ministry have focused on the question of his identity. His teachings and healings have amazed the crowds, and the question "Who is this?" has been raised frequently (7:49; 8:25; 9:9). So, in response to the first question of Jesus, "Who do the crowds say that I am?" the disciples offer the opinions frequently expressed by the people that Jesus must be some kind of prophet. These responses are not so much wrong—Jesus is indeed a great prophet of God— but they are incomplete. Then, the next question of Jesus asks who the disciples have come to understand Jesus to be: "But who do you say that I am?" Peter answers, again speaking for all the disciples, "The Messiah of God." What had been predicted about Jesus in the infancy narratives of the gospel is becoming a part of the disciples' discernment. Their perception of Jesus now matches, at least in part, that of the angels and the demons (2:11; 4:41). Although the disciples' understanding of Jesus still needs to grow, they now understand that Jesus is the Messiah, the promised deliverer sent from God.

With this profession of the disciples' faith, Luke's gospel shifts. Up until this point, the gospel has focused on the proclamation of God's kingdom and on the wonderful displays of Jesus' authority and power. But now attention turns to Jesus instructing his disciples about his mission and what it means for them to be a part of it. His way of delivering people is not what they expect, nor is the way of following him what they expect. He immediately begins to teach them about the full scope of his saving work.

Urging his disciples to silence about Peter's profession of faith, Jesus begins to teach them about the kind of Messiah he is and on what is in store for those who follow in his way. Jesus does not want his disciples making verbal claims about his messianic identity until they understand the nature of his messiahship. He immediately tells them that he must undergo great suffering, rejection, and death, which he sees as integral to his mission. The road of glory runs through the cross. In the midst of what seems to be failure, God is at work in Jesus. In his weakness is his strength. In his humble humanity is his divine mission.

Following Jesus, "the Messiah of God," is more demanding than believing in one who can heal the sick, cast out demons, raise the dead, calm storms, and multiply food. The cost of discipleship is to follow in his way: take up the cross "daily" (verse 23). Only Luke includes the word "daily" in this saying of Jesus. He wants disciples to be clear that following him is a matter for everyday life, a day-by-day expression of perseverance, steadfastness, and faithfulness. Only those who lose their own lives, through self-denial and cross-bearing, will receive life and find salvation (verse 24). Despite its difficulties, the life of a disciple is lived in the hope of glory.

Luke continually emphasizes that prayer is the context for understanding who Jesus is and what it means to be his disciple. He shows Jesus at prayer when he asks his disciples, "Who do you say that I am?" Eight days later Jesus takes his disciples up the mountain to pray, and he is at prayer when his disciples witness his transfigured glory (verses 28-29). More than any other evangelist, Luke demonstrates that deepening faith in Jesus is a result of a prayerful contemplation of his life. Luke is also the only evangelist to include the topic of conversation between Jesus, Moses, and Elijah at the transfiguration: they "were speaking of his departure" (literally, his exodus), "which he was about to accomplish at Jerusalem" (verse 31). Jesus is the new and greater Moses: more radiant than Moses on the mountain (Exod 34:29), a prophet like Moses to whom his people must listen (Deut 18:15), whose exodus—his passion, death, resurrection, and ascension—will be the foundational event for the new and greater Israel. As the divine voice identifies Jesus as "my Son, my Chosen," Peter and James and John—and all disciples—are urged to "listen to him!" (verse 35).

Reflection and discussion

• What is the cost to me of following Jesus each day?

• How can people gain the whole world but lose or forfeit themselves (verse 25)? How does what the world offers compare to the advantages of discipleship?

• After the disciples encounter the transfigured Jesus and the heavenly voice commands them to "listen to him," the disciples remain silent. Why is silence the appropriate response to this experience?

Prayer

Lord of glory, I choose to follow in the way of your cross as the path to glory. Give me faith to understand Jesus as the suffering Messiah, and help me to be silent and listen to him as I travel with him to Jerusalem.

"Whoever welcomes this child in my name welcomes me,
and whoever welcomes me welcomes the one who sent me;
for the least among all of you is the greatest." Luke 9:48

Failures of the Disciples

LUKE 9:37-50 ³⁷*On the next day, when they had come down from the mountain, a great crowd met him. ³⁸Just then a man from the crowd shouted, "Teacher, I beg you to look at my son; he is my only child. ³⁹Suddenly a spirit seizes him, and all at once he shrieks. It convulses him until he foams at the mouth; it mauls him and will scarcely leave him. ⁴⁰I begged your disciples to cast it out, but they could not." ⁴¹Jesus answered, "You faithless and perverse generation, how much longer must I be with you and bear with you? Bring your son here." ⁴²While he was coming, the demon dashed him to the ground in convulsions. But Jesus rebuked the unclean spirit, healed the boy, and gave him back to his father. ⁴³And all were astounded at the greatness of God.*

While everyone was amazed at all that he was doing, he said to his disciples, ⁴⁴"Let these words sink into your ears: The Son of Man is going to be betrayed into human hands." ⁴⁵But they did not understand this saying; its meaning was concealed from them, so that they could not perceive it. And they were afraid to ask him about this saying.

⁴⁶An argument arose among them as to which one of them was the greatest. ⁴⁷But Jesus, aware of their inner thoughts, took a little child and put it by his side, ⁴⁸and said to them, "Whoever welcomes this child in my name welcomes me, and whoever welcomes me welcomes the one who sent me; for the least among all of you is the greatest."

⁴⁹*John answered, "Master, we saw someone casting out demons in your name, and we tried to stop him, because he does not follow with us."* ⁵⁰*But Jesus said to him, "Do not stop him; for whoever is not against you is for you."*

These scenes focus on the inadequacies of Jesus' disciples. They have much more to learn about Jesus, so they must listen and be taught by him. Here they fail to perform an exorcism, they fail to understand Jesus' words about suffering and betrayal, and they must learn the meaning of true greatness and collaboration. Each scene shows Jesus instructing his disciples and subjecting the disciples to continual correction, as he prepares them for the role they will assume in Jerusalem.

After the mountaintop experience, the disciples must descend with Jesus and there encounter another crowd scene. A man from the crowd seeks the attention of Jesus and tries to get relief for his tortured son who is possessed by a demon. The father states that he had begged the disciples to cast the spirit out of him, but they were not able. Jesus seems exasperated at his disciples because they are slow learners. They have not put their trust in him and in his power working through them. Despite the fact that Jesus has given them power and authority over all demons and diseases, they are still unable to deliver the boy from evil. The father turns to Jesus to do what his disciples could not. Jesus rebukes the demon, heals the boy, and gives him back to his father.

Jesus receives the usual response of amazement from the crowd, yet Jesus knows that all of that is about to change. The popular adulations form a sharp contrast to Jesus' warning to his disciples that he would be betrayed (verses 43-44). To catch his disciples' attention, Jesus says, "Let these words sink into your ears." Jesus is challenging their thinking about how the Messiah would deliver God's people. Jesus knew the direction his ministry was going, so he begins the process of preparing his disciples.

Yet, the disciples fail to understand. They are unable to grasp what Jesus is saying to them and are afraid to ask. Instead, in an amazing contrast, the disciples argue over their relative importance in the unfolding work of Jesus, disputing over "which one of them was the greatest" (verse 46). After Jesus has told them that he must suffer and be betrayed, and that following him means self-denial and cross-bearing, the disciples are competing for status. Clearly they are not listening well, and his words are not sinking into their ears.

Jesus dramatically makes his point about discipleship by placing a child beside him. The child is too small to think about self-importance. Rather, the child is eager to listen carefully and learn. Like a child, a disciple must learn to depend on God for everything. Jesus is teaching his disciples, in this very visual way, that their "greatness" does not come from themselves, but from their relationship with him and from the role they have been given in the mission of God's kingdom. Among his disciples, everyone counts and no one can be neglected.

The final lesson on discipleship comes as the disciples tell Jesus that they tried to prevent someone from ministering in his name because he was not from their own inner circle (verse 49). But Jesus states clearly that anyone who is not opposed to the disciples but is working alongside them is sharing in their task. There is no place for jealousy and rivalry among those who wish to serve the kingdom. Jesus calls them to cooperation and collaboration, for many coworkers are needed for the work to be done.

This concludes a major section of Luke's gospel, narrating the ministry of Jesus in Galilee. The focus has been on the identity of Jesus through his preaching and healing. But now that the disciples are able to identify Jesus as the Messiah of God, Jesus will begin to move toward Jerusalem. The disciples lack understanding, so Jesus has much to teach them about the type of Messiah he is and the type of discipleship he desires from them.

Reflection and discussion

• In what ways do you notice the focus of the gospel shifting in these passages?

• Why were the disciples unable to expel an unclean spirit despite having received a share of Jesus' power and authority?

• In what ways are the characteristics of greatness for disciples different from the criteria of worldly success?

• In what ways do rivalry and competitiveness hinder the work of discipleship?

Prayer

Lord God, you protect me from evil and, through Jesus, you give me the power and authority to confront the evil around me. Though I am as powerless as a child, help me to depend on you for my strength and trust in your grace.

SUGGESTIONS FOR FACILITATORS, GROUP SESSION 5

1. Welcome group members and ask if anyone has any questions, announcements, or requests.

2. You may want to pray this prayer as a group:

Lord and Father, Peter confessed Jesus to be the Messiah of God, and from the mountain you proclaimed Jesus your Chosen Son. We have witnessed his authority over the oppressive powers of the sea, demons, disease, and even death, and we know that he has compassion on all who turn to him in need. Help us learn to listen carefully to him, as he teaches us about the kind of Messiah he is and about how to be his disciple. May your word find a receptive and generous heart within us so that we can bear fruit for your kingdom.

3. Ask one or more of the following questions:
   • What most intrigued you from this week's study?
   • What makes you want to know and understand more of God's word?

4. Discuss lessons 19 through 24. Choose one or more of the questions for reflection and discussion from each lesson to talk over as a group.

5. Ask the group members to name one thing they have most appreciated about the way the group has worked during this Bible study. Ask group members to discuss any changes they might suggest in the way the group works in future studies.

6. Invite group members to complete lessons 25 through 30 on their own during the six days before the next meeting. They should write out their own answers to the questions as preparation for next week's session.

7. Ask group members what they find most fascinating about the ministry of Jesus in Luke's gospel. Discuss some of these insights in Luke's presentation of Jesus.

8. Conclude by praying aloud together the prayer at the end of one of the lessons discussed. You may want to conclude the prayer by asking members to voice prayers of thanksgiving.

"No one who puts a hand to the plow and looks back is fit for the kingdom of God." Luke 9:62

The Journey to Jerusalem Begins

LUKE 9:51-62 ⁵¹*When the days drew near for him to be taken up, he set his face to go to Jerusalem. ⁵²And he sent messengers ahead of him. On their way they entered a village of the Samaritans to make ready for him; ⁵³but they did not receive him, because his face was set toward Jerusalem. ⁵⁴When his disciples James and John saw it, they said, "Lord, do you want us to command fire to come down from heaven and consume them?" ⁵⁵But he turned and rebuked them. ⁵⁶Then they went on to another village.*

⁵⁷As they were going along the road, someone said to him, "I will follow you wherever you go." ⁵⁸And Jesus said to him, "Foxes have holes, and birds of the air have nests; but the Son of Man has nowhere to lay his head." ⁵⁹To another he said, "Follow me." But he said, "Lord, first let me go and bury my father." ⁶⁰But Jesus said to him, "Let the dead bury their own dead; but as for you, go and proclaim the kingdom of God." ⁶¹Another said, "I will follow you, Lord; but let me first say farewell to those at my home." ⁶²Jesus said to him, "No one who puts a hand to the plow and looks back is fit for the kingdom of God."

L uke's gospel has reached a turning point as Jesus "set his face to go to Jerusalem." This description of Jesus' resolve indicates that he is absolutely determined to journey toward the city where he will complete his mission. A new major section of the gospel begins here and continues until Jesus enters Jerusalem. Less concerned with powerful preaching and mighty deeds, this journey to Jerusalem focuses on the teachings of Jesus as he forms his disciples for the tasks ahead.

Traveling southward from Galilee and nearing Samaria, Jesus and his disciples encounter resistance. Because Jesus is traveling with a sizable group of disciples, he sends messengers ahead to prepare the townspeople for his arrival and to arrange accommodations. But the Samaritans refuse to receive him "because his face was set toward Jerusalem." Walls of division and bitter hatred divided the Samaritans and the Jews. The Samaritans were descendants of Israel's northern tribes who were conquered by the Assyrians centuries before. The Jews believed that the Samaritans compromised their religion and contaminated their race with foreigners. Most Jews preferred to go around Samaria when going between Galilee and Judea, but Jesus does not avoid Samaria and offers them an opportunity to receive him.

When James and John saw the rejection of Jesus by the Samaritans, their instinctual response was to send a destructive judgment on the village (verse 54). The consuming fire from heaven is an allusion to the destruction that Elijah visited upon the enemies of Israel (2 Kings 1:10, 12). Of course, Jesus rebukes them because their zeal is completely misguided for disciples who have been taught to love their enemies and do good for those who hate them. Jesus has already instructed them how to respond to unwelcoming villages by telling them to shake the dust from their feet. They must move on and offer the gospel to others. The act of judgment is left to God alone. The fire from heaven would come after the ascension of Jesus—not a consuming fire, but the transforming fire of the Holy Spirit.

After the experience of rejection, Jesus continues to teach about the demands of discipleship through his encounter with three would-be disciples. The first volunteers to follow Jesus wherever he may go. To this open-ended declaration, Jesus responds with frankness about what such a commitment would mean. The proverb Jesus quotes expresses his "homelessness" in the world (verse 58). Following him means living like Jesus, as a stranger in the world and experiencing rejection from many. Discipleship is a reorientation of life, being ready to face risk and suffering.

The second prospective disciple wants to follow Jesus, but he comes up with a reason to delay his response. Unlike the fishermen and the tax collector, who immediately left all to follow Jesus, this man wishes to wait until his father dies and his family duties are behind him. While this seems like a reasonable request, the reply of Jesus stresses the urgency of proclaiming God's kingdom (verse 60). Many would-be followers of Jesus have pleaded the requirements of business demands, social obligations, and even family responsibilities, but Jesus teaches that nothing is to block the pursuit of discipleship or postpone its start.

The third possible disciple states that he will follow Jesus, but first desires to bid farewell to his family. The request parallels Elisha's response when Elijah calls him to follow. Elisha kisses his mother and father before following the prophet (1 Kings 19:19-21). Jesus' reply suggests that disciples must have the urgency and commitment of Elisha, who not only bid farewell to his parents but also offered up his oxen in sacrifice, using the wood of his plow for fuel. Using the metaphor of the plow, Jesus teaches that a disciple must keep his eye focused on following Jesus and not look back (verse 62). Like a farmer who must plow with eyes directly ahead so that he plows a straight furrow, the disciple must always give his attention to God's call.

We don't know whether these three became disciples or not. But the teachings of Jesus directed to them offer directions for all seeking to follow in his way. For the disciple, the highest priority is the kingdom of God. All other obligations and desires pale in comparison. Following Jesus is a solemn commitment to follow one whom the world does not embrace. It means breaking with the ways of one's past and often severing old ties. Walking in the path of Jesus involves one's whole life. The path is not easy, but discipleship means looking ahead with singular dedication to the work of the kingdom.

Reflection and discussion

• What can I expect to learn in this new section of the gospel as Jesus travels toward Jerusalem?

• Why did Jesus choose to travel through Samaria and not around it? What does this choice teach me about him?

• What are some of the obstacles that hold people back from the real commitment of being disciples of Jesus?

• What is so all-consuming and urgent about the call to be a disciple of Jesus? How do I respond to his call?

Prayer

Heavenly Father, the call to follow in the way of your Son is your appeal to reorient my life. Show me the obstacles that hold me back from being a disciple so that I may wholeheartedly follow Jesus.

"The harvest is plentiful, but the laborers are few;
therefore ask the Lord of the harvest
to send out laborers into his harvest. Go on your way." Luke 10:2-3

Acceptance and Rejection
of the Mission

LUKE 10:1-20 *¹After this the Lord appointed seventy others and sent them on ahead of him in pairs to every town and place where he himself intended to go. ²He said to them, "The harvest is plentiful, but the laborers are few; therefore ask the Lord of the harvest to send out laborers into his harvest. ³Go on your way. See, I am sending you out like lambs into the midst of wolves. ⁴Carry no purse, no bag, no sandals; and greet no one on the road. ⁵Whatever house you enter, first say, 'Peace to this house!' ⁶And if anyone is there who shares in peace, your peace will rest on that person; but if not, it will return to you. ⁷Remain in the same house, eating and drinking whatever they provide, for the laborer deserves to be paid. Do not move about from house to house. ⁸Whenever you enter a town and its people welcome you, eat what is set before you; ⁹cure the sick who are there, and say to them, 'The kingdom of God has come near to you.' ¹⁰But whenever you enter a town and they do not welcome you, go out into its streets and say, ¹¹'Even the dust of your town that clings to our feet, we wipe off in protest against you. Yet know this: the kingdom of God has come near.' ¹²I tell you, on that day it will be more tolerable for Sodom than for that town.*

¹³"Woe to you, Chorazin! Woe to you, Bethsaida! For if the deeds of power done in you had been done in Tyre and Sidon, they would have repented long ago, sitting in sackcloth and ashes. ¹⁴But at the judgment it will be more tolerable for Tyre and Sidon than for you. ¹⁵And you, Capernaum,

will you be exalted to heaven?

No, you will be brought down to Hades.

¹⁶*"Whoever listens to you listens to me, and whoever rejects you rejects me, and whoever rejects me rejects the one who sent me."*

¹⁷*The seventy returned with joy, saying, "Lord, in your name even the demons submit to us!" ¹⁸He said to them, "I watched Satan fall from heaven like a flash of lightning. ¹⁹See, I have given you authority to tread on snakes and scorpions, and over all the power of the enemy; and nothing will hurt you. ²⁰Nevertheless, do not rejoice at this, that the spirits submit to you, but rejoice that your names are written in heaven."*

Jesus appoints a number of his disciples outside of the Twelve to go ahead of him to prepare the regions where he intends to go. The number Jesus appoints is seventy (or seventy-two in some manuscripts), and he tells them to travel in pairs for mutual support. Like the number twelve, seventy is also related to the origins of Israel. During the journey of exodus, God told Moses to gather seventy of the elders of Israel (Num 11:16-17). These seventy received some of the spirit God had given to Moses, and they assisted Moses in leading the people. These seventy disciples of Jesus represent him when he is absent, and they carry out what will be the work of the church.

The successful missionary work of Jesus and his disciples is depicted as a plentiful harvest. Although they sometimes experience rejection, there is still much positive response to the gospel. Yet there are not enough laborers to reap the harvest, so Jesus tells his disciples to ask God, "the Lord of the harvest," to call forth more men and women to serve with them so that the missionary task will grow. As people receive the gospel they will take responsibility for it and help deliver it to others.

Jesus sends them out on a mission that is filled with risk. They go as vulnerable lambs into the midst of wolves, but always by his authority and as his representatives. They must travel light and single-mindedly press on to their goal, without a hint of pretension, while relying on God's help and protection. Jesus explains that when they enter a house, they must extend a blessing of peace, offering God's grace, mercy, and salvation (verse 5). If the blessing is received with an open heart, it extends God's peace to the receiver. If it is rejected, it returns to the sender so that it can be given to someone more receptive (verse 6). The blessings brought by the laborers for God's kingdom are worthy of a wage of food and shelter from those who receive them (verse 7). And, lastly, Jesus tells these disciples how to respond to acceptance and how to respond to rejection.

The message of these disciples for those who receive them is this: "The kingdom of God has come near to you." With the coming of Jesus, God's reign is at hand, and healing the sick by the disciples is one manifestation of its approach. In these initial phases of the kingdom's fulfillment, God extends his saving power upon people in the face of all opposing forces. It is inaugurated in the coming of the Messiah, and God's future reign is guaranteed. Nothing can stop God's kingdom from coming. The signs of the kingdom are here. It is time to receive it and enter into God's reign.

People can refuse God's offer of salvation, but it is the worst form of neglect. Those who reject God's offer of deliverance from the effects of sin and death will experience inevitable judgment. Jesus expresses another set of prophetic woes (see also 6:24-26), this time directed to the cities in which people failed to respond to the gospel proclaimed by Jesus and his disciples (verse 13). Warning of the nearness and danger of judgment and calling them to repentance, Jesus exclaims his anguish and pity for those who refuse the salvation he offers. In fact, Sodom, Tyre, and Sidon, notoriously wicked cities condemned by the ancient prophets, are better off than Chorazin, Bethsaida, and Capernaum, who refused God's offer of grace and failed to respond to the gospel of God's kingdom. The stinging rebuke emphasizes how sin can blind people in the face of God's mercy and forgiveness.

When they return to Jesus, the seventy are rejoicing over the success of their mission (verse 17). They address Jesus as Lord and acknowledge that they have ministered in his name. Even demons are subject to them because they represent Jesus and share in his power. In a prophetic vision, Jesus sees Satan fall from heaven like a flash of lightning. Clearly, the disciples' ministry spells defeat for Satan. In fact, the disciples can overcome anything that opposes them through the authority of Jesus. The power of the evil one cannot remove their secure position before God nor erase their names from God's book of life.

Reflection and discussion

• How are Christian disciples called to be laborers for the harvest of God's kingdom?

• What are some indications that the reign of God is a reality in a person's life?

• What is my deepest source of joy? When has an awareness of what God was doing through me brought me joy?

Prayer

Lord of the harvest, you send out laborers to reap the harvest of your kingdom. I rejoice that I serve in the name of the Lord Jesus, that the powers of evil are defeated, and that my name is written in heaven.

"Blessed are the eyes that see what you see! For I tell you that many prophets and kings desired to see what you see, but did not see it, and to hear what you hear, but did not hear it." Luke 10:23-24

The Compassionate Samaritan

LUKE 10:21-42 ²¹*At that same hour Jesus rejoiced in the Holy Spirit and said, "I thank you, Father, Lord of heaven and earth, because you have hidden these things from the wise and the intelligent and have revealed them to infants; yes, Father, for such was your gracious will. ²²All things have been handed over to me by my Father; and no one knows who the Son is except the Father, or who the Father is except the Son and anyone to whom the Son chooses to reveal him."*

²³Then turning to the disciples, Jesus said to them privately, "Blessed are the eyes that see what you see! ²⁴For I tell you that many prophets and kings desired to see what you see, but did not see it, and to hear what you hear, but did not hear it."

²⁵Just then a lawyer stood up to test Jesus. "Teacher," he said, "what must I do to inherit eternal life?" ²⁶He said to him, "What is written in the law? What do you read there?" ²⁷He answered, "You shall love the Lord your God with all your heart, and with all your soul, and with all your strength, and with all your mind; and your neighbor as yourself." ²⁸And he said to him, "You have given the right answer; do this, and you will live."

²⁹But wanting to justify himself, he asked Jesus, "And who is my neighbor?"

119

30Jesus replied, "A man was going down from Jerusalem to Jericho, and fell into the hands of robbers, who stripped him, beat him, and went away, leaving him half dead. 31Now by chance a priest was going down that road; and when he saw him, he passed by on the other side. 32So likewise a Levite, when he came to the place and saw him, passed by on the other side. 33But a Samaritan while traveling came near him; and when he saw him, he was moved with pity. 34He went to him and bandaged his wounds, having poured oil and wine on them. Then he put him on his own animal, brought him to an inn, and took care of him. 35The next day he took out two denarii, gave them to the innkeeper, and said, 'Take care of him; and when I come back, I will repay you whatever more you spend.' 36Which of these three, do you think, was a neighbor to the man who fell into the hands of the robbers?" 37He said, "The one who showed him mercy." Jesus said to him, "Go and do likewise."

38Now as they went on their way, he entered a certain village, where a woman named Martha welcomed him into her home. 39She had a sister named Mary, who sat at the Lord's feet and listened to what he was saying. 40But Martha was distracted by her many tasks; so she came to him and asked, "Lord, do you not care that my sister has left me to do all the work by myself? Tell her then to help me." 41But the Lord answered her, "Martha, Martha, you are worried and distracted by many things; 42there is need of only one thing. Mary has chosen the better part, which will not be taken away from her."

The scene expresses deep joy and wonder as Jesus continues to form his disciples. His spontaneous prayer expresses his gratitude to the Father for revealing the ways of the kingdom to those who are simple and openhearted, unimpeded by preconceived ideas of how God should act. God's "gracious will" has always worked in this way: resisting the proud and giving grace to the humble. Although God freely gives, the attitude of the receiver determines the internal effects of that grace. The Father has entrusted everything to his Son, so Jesus is the channel of God's revelation and can make him known to anyone. No one can truly understand the Father's saving will without listening to his Son. The prophets and kings of ancient Israel longed to see and hear the wonders of this age of salvation brought by Jesus. How honored and blessed are all disciples who live in the time of fulfillment!

The parable of the good Samaritan and the account of Martha and

Mary are unique to Luke's gospel. The people in these scenes are characters in whom we can see our own flaws: the lawyer trying to justify himself (verses 25, 29), priest and Levite too concerned with their own needs (verses 31-32), and Martha plagued with anxiety and resentment (verses 40-41). The surprising heroes of the stories are those who exhibit genuine love (verse 27): the despised Samaritan who, despite great personal risk, stopped to care for the injured traveler (verse 34), and Mary, who received the traveling Jesus, listening and learning from him (verse 39).

The lawyer's question asks what he must do to receive all that God has to offer him. Jesus sends the lawyer to God's instructions for his people found in the Torah so that he can answer his own question. The lawyer quotes two biblical verses: the first command is to love God with one's whole being (Deut 6:5), and the second is to love one's neighbor as one's self (Lev 19:18). This unified law of love indicates that both devotion to God and care for the neighbor have the same force and cannot be separated (verse 27). The approving response of Jesus emphasizes that this love is not just an abstract feeling but is manifested in concrete responsiveness: "Do this and you will live" (verse 28).

In response, the lawyer wishes to determine the minimal response necessary to comply with the law to love one's neighbor. In ancient Israel, a "neighbor" was a fellow countryman, a member of the covenant. The lawyer knows that if loving his neighbor is the way to life, he wants as few neighbors as possible. However, the parable of the priest, Levite, and compassionate Samaritan teaches that neighborliness is not found in a racial, religious, or national bond. The essence of being a neighbor is having the sensitivity to see a person in need and to act to meet the need. The Samaritan, despised by many Jews of the day, cares for a person he has never seen before, not only soothing the beaten man's wounds, but also taking him to a place of shelter, caring for him, and making sure his needs are met.

While Jesus and his disciples continue on their way, they come to the village of Martha and Mary. The traveling band of men and women depended on the hospitality of such people for food and lodging. But while Martha is busy with all the details, Jesus is teaching in her own home and she doesn't hear a word of it. In contrast, her sister Mary "sat at the Lord's feet and listened to what he was saying" (verse 39). While Martha is "worried and distracted by many things," Jesus says, "There is need of only one thing. Mary has chosen the better part" (verse 42). Martha's anxiety about many things distracts her from the one thing necessary, which is centering her heart on Jesus, listening to him, hearing the word of God. This is what Mary is doing so well.

Reflection and discussion

• How does Jesus teach that love of God is expressed through a life that is sensitive and compassionate to others?

• How does Jesus use a shocking twist in his parable of the priest, Levite, and Samaritan? Why would this have such an impact on his listeners?

• In what ways do I see both Martha and Mary mirrored in my discipleship? How do I strike an appropriate balance between the doing of Martha and the listening of Mary?

Prayer

Lord of heaven and earth, I am blessed to experience what ancient prophets and kings only longed for. Thank you for revealing your kingdom to me and for the privilege of living in the time of Christ's church. Give me the grace to sit and listen to your word and to respond with wholehearted care for my neighbor.

"So I say to you, Ask, and it will be given you; search, and you will find; knock, and the door will be opened for you." Luke 11:9

The Teaching of Jesus on Prayer

LUKE 11:1-13 *¹He was praying in a certain place, and after he had finished, one of his disciples said to him, "Lord, teach us to pray, as John taught his disciples." ²He said to them, "When you pray, say:*

Father, hallowed be your name.

Your kingdom come.

³Give us each day our daily bread.

⁴And forgive us our sins,

for we ourselves forgive everyone indebted to us.

And do not bring us to the time of trial."

⁵And he said to them, "Suppose one of you has a friend, and you go to him at midnight and say to him, 'Friend, lend me three loaves of bread; ⁶for a friend of mine has arrived, and I have nothing to set before him.' ⁷And he answers from within, 'Do not bother me; the door has already been locked, and my children are with me in bed; I cannot get up and give you anything.' ⁸I tell you, even though he will not get up and give him anything because he is his friend, at least because of his persistence he will get up and give him whatever he needs.

⁹"So I say to you, Ask, and it will be given you; search, and you will find; knock, and the door will be opened for you. ¹⁰For everyone who asks receives, and everyone who searches finds, and for everyone who knocks, the door will be opened. ¹¹*Is there anyone among you who, if your child asks for a fish, will give a snake instead of a fish?* ¹²*Or if the child asks for an egg, will give a scorpion?* ¹³*If you then, who are evil, know how to give good gifts to your children, how much more will the heavenly Father give the Holy Spirit to those who ask him!"*

Throughout Luke's gospel, we see Jesus at prayer. There must have been something particularly attractive about the way Jesus prayed that made his disciples ask Jesus to teach them to pray. In response Jesus offers them a model prayer (verses 2-4), a parable about asking for what they need (verses 5-8), and an encouragement about how to approach God with confidence when they pray (verses 9-13). In all these teachings, Jesus uses terms and images drawn from family life to show that God is a loving Father to his daughters and sons.

The model prayer that Jesus offers invites us to address God in familial terms, "Father," to participate in his own intimate relationship with God. What should we pray for? First, we ask that God's name be sanctified and held in reverence. We can bring honor to God's good name or we can disgrace his reputation by the things we say and do. Second, we pray for the fullness of God's kingdom. Since the kingdom has been inaugurated with the coming of Jesus, our lives can manifest God's reign in the world while we await its fullness. The third petition requests that God grant us what we need to sustain us in all aspects of our lives. Yet, since "daily bread" can also be translated as "bread for tomorrow" or "bread that is coming," the petition asks God to bring us to the banquet of his eternal kingdom. Fourth, we ask God to forgive our sins and the debt we owe when we sin against others. Finally, we pray that we be kept safe during times of testing, temptation, or enticement to sin. So we ask God to help us stand firm in the midst of whatever trial or suffering comes our way.

Jesus' parable asks that his disciples envision a situation that would not have been at all difficult to imagine at the time. People often traveled at night to avoid the heat of the day, so an unexpected visitor at midnight would not be uncommon. And since Palestinian homes were small, often with a mat serving as a bed for the whole family, it would not be difficult to understand why the friend would not want to get up and disturb the whole family. With this brief parable, Jesus teaches that God will answer our prayers. If a person will answer the request of a friend, though not eagerly because of great inconvenience, certainly God, for whom there is no inconvenient time, will answer the prayers of his children.

Jesus concludes his teaching by instructing his disciples to ask, to search, and to know, knowing that when we ask we will receive, when we search we will find, and when we knock the door will be opened (verses 9-10). In other words, we should pray expectantly, knowing that God always responds to our prayers. When children ask for the necessities of life like a fish or an egg, what parent would refuse them, or give them a snake or a scorpion instead (verses 11-12)? If even imperfect earthly parents do good in response to their children's requests, how much more will our heavenly Father give to those who ask!

We should imitate the expectancy of children who are not afraid to ask their parents for anything because they know they can count completely on their love. God delights in answering our prayers and giving us good things. In fact, God gives us the best gift of all, the Holy Spirit, the one in whom we share in God's very life (verse 13).

Reflection and discussion

• Notice the number of times Jesus' model prayer contains the word "us." What do the words of this prayer teach the disciples about the communal nature of prayer?

• What is the meaning of the prayer petition, "hallowed be your name"? How can what I say and do "hallow" the name of God?

• What have the parable and teachings of Jesus helped me learn about prayer?

• Do I pray with confidence? With trust? With persistence? With expectancy? How can I pray better?

Prayer

God my Father, help me to pray to you with all the trust of an eager child, knowing that I will receive good things from you. May I pray the prayer that Jesus taught us with new confidence and expectancy, trusting in you as my loving parent.

"Every kingdom divided against itself becomes a desert,
and house falls on house. If Satan also is divided against himself,
how will his kingdom stand?" Luke 11:17-18

The Two Kingdoms

LUKE 11:14-26 ¹⁴*Now he was casting out a demon that was mute; when the demon had gone out, the one who had been mute spoke, and the crowds were amazed. ¹⁵But some of them said, "He casts out demons by Beelzebul, the ruler of the demons." ¹⁶Others, to test him, kept demanding from him a sign from heaven. ¹⁷But he knew what they were thinking and said to them, "Every kingdom divided against itself becomes a desert, and house falls on house. ¹⁸If Satan also is divided against himself, how will his kingdom stand? —for you say that I cast out the demons by Beelzebul. ¹⁹Now if I cast out the demons by Beelzebul, by whom do your exorcists cast them out? Therefore they will be your judges. ²⁰But if it is by the finger of God that I cast out the demons, then the kingdom of God has come to you. ²¹When a strong man, fully armed, guards his castle, his property is safe. ²²But when one stronger than he attacks him and overpowers him, he takes away his armor in which he trusted and divides his plunder. ²³Whoever is not with me is against me, and whoever does not gather with me scatters.*

²⁴*"When the unclean spirit has gone out of a person, it wanders through waterless regions looking for a resting place, but not finding any, it says, 'I will return to my house from which I came.' ²⁵When it comes, it finds it swept and put in order. ²⁶Then it goes and brings seven other spirits more evil than itself,*

and they enter and live there; and the last state of that person is worse than the first."

A fter teaching us the Lord's prayer, the gospel now focuses on the Lord's power. The conflict of power is between two kingdoms, that of Satan and that of God. Those who oppose God's kingdom do not pray as Jesus taught. Rather than asking with trusting confidence, they seek a sign from heaven (verse 16). Rather than praying for the coming of God's kingdom, they accuse Jesus of being aligned with the reign of Satan (verse 15). Rather than asking for forgiveness of their sins, they accuse Jesus of sinning under the influence of the evil one. Rather than praying to be delivered from testing, they put Jesus to the test.

The healing of the mute man, the result, and the response are narrated quickly. Jesus casts out the demon, the mute man is able to speak, and the crowds are amazed (verse 14). But debate and skepticism about the work of Jesus follow. The fact that Jesus performs amazing works is evident to all, so the source of his power must be either divine or demonic. Some attribute the expulsion of the demon to the power of Beelzebul, the ruler of the demons. Others were not quite so cynical but they demand to see a sign that proves he is from God.

Jesus responds with a proverb stating that a kingdom divided against itself cannot stand (verse 17). In other words, if the members of a realm are at odds with one another, civil war results and the kingdom is destroyed from within. Jesus says that if Satan is casting out his own demons, then his realm is divided against itself—a sure formula for collapse (verse 18). So it seems illogical that Jesus and the others who exorcise demons would be working through demonic power. Since Satan's influence is seen in disease, demonic possession, and death, the reversal of this destruction cannot be the work of Satan.

Jesus proclaims instead that, since he is casting out demons through the power of God, the kingdom of God has come upon them (verse 20). The prophetic hope that God would bring to pass the promised age is fulfilled, and Jesus' mighty acts give evidence of the arrival of the kingdom. The battle between Jesus and Satan is a cosmic struggle. Satan is pictured as a strong man, secure in his castle, yet fully armed and ready to defend his realm (verse 21). But Jesus is "one stronger than he," who attacks and overpowers Satan.

The victory of Jesus is graphically described as he strips away the armor of Satan's power and releases those held in his captivity so that they can enter the kingdom of God.

This demonstration of Jesus' saving authority forces everyone to a decision about who he is, and the decision about his identity determines how they respond to him. Those who choose to follow Jesus join with him in bringing others into the kingdom, reaping the harvest of salvation. Those who turn away from him influence others to turn away from him, scattering the harvest and working against the salvation that God desires for all.

Jesus concludes with a final image, convincing those who experience God's saving work to follow up by inviting God to occupy their lives (verses 24-26). When a demonic spirit is expelled by God's power, it wanders looking for a place to dwell and will often return to the house from which it came. When the evil one finds it empty and prepared for a guest, he brings seven other evil spirits and occupies the house. Through this haunting image, Jesus warns that those who experience God's work within them must follow up with firm faith, allowing God's Spirit to fill them. Those who leave their souls a vacuum or in spiritual neutral remain in peril, but those who continue to listen to God's word and follow Jesus are secure in their blessedness.

Reflection and discussion

• What are some signs that I am now living under God's rule rather than that of the evil one?

• How does Jesus show the foolishness of the claim that he works through the power of Satan?

• Why is there no neutral ground when it comes to a choice for or against Jesus? How does Jesus emphasize the critical significance of that choice?

• What is Jesus teaching me through the image of the house occupied by demons?

Prayer

Lord God, you invite all people to live in your reign. Today I renounce Satan with all his works, and I seek to bear witness to your kingdom in what I say and do. Help me to develop a strong house of faith that is kept safe from attack and plunder.

"Just as Jonah became a sign to the people of Nineveh, so the Son of Man will be to this generation." Luke 11:30

True Blessedness

LUKE 11:27-36 ²⁷*While he was saying this, a woman in the crowd raised her voice and said to him, "Blessed is the womb that bore you and the breasts that nursed you!" ²⁸But he said, "Blessed rather are those who hear the word of God and obey it!"*

²⁹When the crowds were increasing, he began to say, "This generation is an evil generation; it asks for a sign, but no sign will be given to it except the sign of Jonah. ³⁰For just as Jonah became a sign to the people of Nineveh, so the Son of Man will be to this generation. ³¹The queen of the South will rise at the judgment with the people of this generation and condemn them, because she came from the ends of the earth to listen to the wisdom of Solomon, and see, something greater than Solomon is here! ³²The people of Nineveh will rise up at the judgment with this generation and condemn it, because they repented at the proclamation of Jonah, and see, something greater than Jonah is here!

³³"No one after lighting a lamp puts it in a cellar, but on the lampstand so that those who enter may see the light. ³⁴Your eye is the lamp of your body. If your eye is healthy, your whole body is full of light; but if it is not healthy, your body is full of darkness. ³⁵Therefore consider whether the light in you is not darkness. ³⁶If then your whole body is full of light, with no part of it in darkness, it will be as full of light as when a lamp gives you light with its rays."

I n contrast to those in the crowd who think Jesus is an agent of Satan or who demand signs from him, a woman in the crowd cries out a beatitude for the womb that bore him and the breasts that nursed him. Since a mother is honored through the accomplishments of her son in Palestinian culture, the praise of Mary is also an expression of gratitude to Jesus. The woman from the crowd echoes the cry of Elizabeth, "Blessed are you among women and blessed is the fruit of your womb" (1:42), and fulfills Mary's prophecy, "From now on all generations will call me blessed" (1:48). In response to the woman's declaration, Jesus offers a beatitude of his own, emphasizing the blessedness of "those who hear the word of God and obey it." The saying summarizes a ce ntral teaching of Jesus expressed throughout the gospel: blessings come to those who both listen to God's word and act on it (6:47; 8:15; 8:21). Although Mary is preeminent among those who listen and respond to God's word, all persons of all times and places are blessed when they hear and obey the word of God.

To those demanding a sign from Jesus, he tells them that no sign will be given "except the sign of Jonah." Just as the prophet Jonah was a sign to the people of Nineveh because he preached God's word to them, Jesus is a sign to the present generation because he proclaims the word of God to them (verse 30). Likewise, the Queen of Sheba traveled to King Solomon to hear God's wisdom spoken from him. The people of Nineveh responded with repentance to the word spoken by Jonah (Jonah 3:5), and the queen responded with praise to the God of Israel for the wisdom spoken through Solomon (1 Kings 10:9). Because these Gentiles responded so favorably to Jonah and Solomon, they show themselves more receptive to God's revelation than the present generation of Israelites. Because Jesus is "greater than Jonah" and "greater than Solomon," the crowd should certainly respond to the word and wisdom of God spoken through Jesus his Son (verses 31-32).

Finally, Jesus turns to the image of light as a metaphor for the revelation of God that Jesus provides by his teaching. An oil lamp must not be lit and then hidden in a cellar, but placed on a lamp stand to be seen by everyone (verse 33). Likewise, Jesus' teachings are not private disclosures, but must be openly proclaimed to all. Jesus then uses a similar image to describe the eye as a lamp for the body (verse 34). In ancient times, the eye was thought of not only as a window that lets in light but as a lamp that gives light to the body. When the eye is healthy, it fills the whole body with light; when it is not healthy, the body remains in darkness. As the spread of light depends on the position of the lamp or the health of the eye, we must keep our lamps in good condition so that the light Jesus offers will illuminate both our inner and outer lives. When our whole body is full of light, we will shine brightly and give off light to others. When we hear the word of God through Jesus and act on it, we will reflect God's truth by the way we live and become instruments of his revelation to others.

Reflection and discussion

• Why does Jesus shift the emphasis from the womb and breasts of his mother to hearing and obeying the word of God?

• How did the Ninevites and Queen of the South respond to the word and wisdom spoken by Jonah and Solomon? In what ways is Jesus "greater" than Jonah and Solomon?

• How can I allow the word of God to make my whole body be full of light? What happens when the teachings of Jesus penetrate my life in this way?

Prayer

Father in heaven, open my ears to hear your word and my eyes to see the light of Christ. As I continue to study the gospel of your Son, give me the grace to act on your word and to illumine the lives of those around me.

SUGGESTIONS FOR FACILITATORS, GROUP SESSION 6

1. Welcome group members and make any final announcements or requests.

2. You may want to pray this prayer as a group:

God of Israel and Father of Jesus, we are blessed to be living in the age of salvation for which the ancient prophets and kings only longed. You have called us to sit at the feet of Jesus to listen to your word and to bear witness to your revelation by all we say and do. Thank you for choosing us to be laborers who reap the harvest of your kingdom in this time of fulfillment. As we continue this journey with Jesus, guide us to understand his teachings and give us a deep desire to be his disciples, sharing in his mission of salvation for the world.

3. Ask one or more of the following questions:
   • How has this study of Luke's gospel enriched your life?
   • In what way has this study challenged you the most?

4. Discuss lessons 25 through 30. Choose one or more of the questions for reflection and discussion from each lesson to discuss as a group.

5. Ask the group if they would like to study another in the Threshold Bible Study series. Discuss the topic and dates, and make a decision among those interested. Ask the group members to suggest people they would like to invite to participate in the next study series.

6. Ask the group to discuss the insights that stand out most from this study over the past six weeks.

7. Conclude by praying aloud the following prayer or another of your own choosing:

Holy Spirit of the living God, you inspired the writers of the Scriptures and you have guided our study during these weeks. Continue to deepen our love for the word of God in the holy Scriptures, and draw us more deeply into the heart of Jesus. We thank you for the confident hope you have placed within us and the gifts that build up the church. Through this study, lead us to worship and witness more fully and fervently, and bless us now and always with the fire of your love.

The
GOSPEL
OF LUKE
in the Sunday Lectionary

LUKE 1:1-4; 4:14-21
3rd Sunday in Ordinary Time
(69C)

LUKE 1:26-38
4th Sunday of Advent
(11-B)

LUKE 1:39-45
4th Sunday of Advent
(12-C)

LUKE 1:46-48, 49-50, 53-54
3rd Sunday of Advent (resp.)
(8-B)

LUKE 2:1-14
Christmas: Mass at Midnight
(14-ABC)

LUKE 2:15-20
Christmas: Mass at Dawn
(15-ABC)

LUKE 2:22-40 OR 2:22, 39-40
Sunday in Octave of Christmas: Holy Family
(17-B)

LUKE 2:41-52
Sunday in Octave of Christmas: Holy Family
(17-C)

LUKE 3:1-6
2nd Sunday of Advent
(6-C)

LUKE 3:10-18
3rd Sunday of Advent
(9-C)

THE GOSPEL OF LUKE IN THE SUNDAY LECTIONARY

LUKE 3:15-16, 21-22
Sunday after Epiphany:
Baptism of the Lord *(21-C)*

LUKE 4:1-13
1st Sunday of Lent
(24-C)

LUKE 4:14-21 (WITH 1:1-4)
3rd Sunday in Ordinary Time
(69-C)

LUKE 4:21-30
4th Sunday in Ordinary Time
(72-C)

LUKE 5:1-11
5th Sunday in Ordinary Time
(75-C)

LUKE 6:17, 20-26
6th Sunday in Ordinary Time
(78-C)

LUKE 6:27-38
7th Sunday in Ordinary Time
(81-C)

LUKE 6:39-45
8th Sunday in Ordinary Time
(84-C)

LUKE 7:1-10
9th Sunday in Ordinary Time
(87-C)

LUKE 7:11-17
10th Sunday in Ordinary Time
(90-C)

LUKE 7:36—8:3 OR 7:36-50
11th Sunday in Ordinary Time
(93-C)

LUKE 9:11B-17
Sunday after Trinity Sun:
Body & Blood of Christ *(169-C)*

LUKE 9:18-24
12th Sunday in Ordinary Time
(96-C)

LUKE 9:28B-36
2nd Sunday of Lent
(27-C)

LUKE 9:51-62
13th Sunday in Ordinary Time
(99-C)

LUKE 10:1-12, 17-20 OR 10:1-9
14th Sunday in Ordinary Time
(102-C)

THE GOSPEL OF LUKE IN THE SUNDAY LECTIONARY

LUKE 17:5-10
27th Sunday in Ordinary Time
(141-C)

LUKE 17:11-19
28th Sunday in Ordinary Time
(144-C)

LUKE 18:1-8
29th Sunday in Ordinary Time
(147-C)

LUKE 18:9-14
30th Sunday in Ordinary Time
(150-C)

LUKE 19:1-10
31st Sunday in Ordinary Time
(153-C)

LUKE 19:28-40
Palm Sunday: Procession of Palms
(37-C)

LUKE 20:27-38 OR 20:27, 34-38
32nd Sunday in Ordinary Time
(156-C)

LUKE 21:5-19
33rd Sunday in Ordinary Time
(159-C)

LUKE 21:25-28, 34-36
1st Sunday of Advent
(3-C)

LUKE 22:14—23:56 OR 23:1-49
Palm Sunday Mass
(38-C)

LUKE 23:35-43
34th Sunday in Ordinary Time:
Christ the King *(162-C)*

LUKE 24:1-12
Easter Vigil
(41-C)

LUKE 24:13-35
Easter Sunday: Resurrection of the Lord
(opt. 2) *(42-ABC)*

LUKE 24:13-35
3rd Sunday of Easter
(46-A)

LUKE 24:35-48
3rd Sunday of Easter
(47-B)

LUKE 24:46-53
Ascension of the Lord
(58-C)

Ordering Additional Studies

TWENTY
THIRD 23rd
PUBLICATIONS

To check availability or for a description
of each study, visit our website at
www.ThresholdBibleStudy.com
or call us at **1-800-321-0411**